THE VAULT DOOR

CINDY LAFAVRE YORKS

TABLE OF CONTENTS

Introduction   ix

WEEK 1: IN THE VAULT
1. In the Vault: Denying Outside Access   3
2. In the Vault: Inventorying Your Valuables   5
3. In the Vault: Keys to a Solid, Fort-Knox Lockup   8
4. In the Vault: Setting Alarms to Discourage   10
   Intrusion
5. In the Vault: Bolstering Your Security   13
6. In the Vault: Surviving Attacks   15
7. In the Vault: Thanking God for His Protection   17

WEEK 2: LAND WORTH SECURING
1. Land Worth Securing: Eden and Its Perfection   21
2. Land Worth Securing: Eden Undone   23
3. Land Worth Securing: Terrain from Egypt to   25
   Exodus
4. Land Worth Securing: The Wilderness   27
5. Land Worth Securing: Inhabiting Earth's   29
   Promised Land
6. Land Worth Securing: The Commission to   31
   Distant Lands
7. Land Worth Securing: The Ultimate Promised   33
   Land

WEEK 3: THE INVESTMENT OF SPIRITUAL
TRAINING
1. The Investment of Spiritual Training: Training   37
   for God
2. The Investment of Spiritual Training: The   39
   Principle of Specificity
3. The Investment of Spiritual Training: The   41
   Principle of Overload

4. The Investment of Spiritual Training: The   43
   Principle of Progression
5. The Investment of Spiritual Training: The   45
   Principle of Accommodation
6. The Investment of Spiritual Training: The   47
   Principle of Reversibility
7. The Investment of Spiritual Training: The   49
   Principle of Rest

WEEK 4: SEVEN KEY VERSES

1. Seven Key Verses: John 3:16   55
2. Seven Key Verses: John 13:34   57
3. Seven Key Verses: Luke 1:37   59
4. Seven Key Verses: Mark 16:15   61
5. Seven Key Verses: Ephesians 3:18–19   63
6. Seven Key Verses: Isaiah 41:10   65
7. Seven Key Verses: Matthew 28:20   67

WEEK 5: INVESTING IN SECURITY

1. Investing in Security: Guard!   71
2. Investing in Security: In Our Final Destination 73
3. Investing in Security: In the Totality of Our   75
   Redemption
4. Investing in Security: In Being Loved   77
5. Investing in Security: In Following the Law   79
6. Investing in Security: In Following His Will   81
7. Investing in Security: In Our Identity in Christ 83

WEEK 6: VALUABLE LESSONS FROM CREATION

1. Valuable Lessons from Creation: The Serpent   87
2. Valuable Lessons from Creation: The Remnant,   89
   Two by Two
3. Valuable Lessons from Creation: Sacrificial   91
   Animals
4. Valuable Lessons from Creation: Jesus's   93
   Bittersweet Donkey Ride
5. Valuable Lessons from Creation: A Rooster's   95
   Reminder

6. Valuable Lessons from Creation: Signs of   97
the Dove

7. Valuable Lessons from Creation: Sheep and Goats   99

WEEK 7: CONTEMPLATING THE AWE OF GOD

1. Contemplating the Awe of God: His Dazzling   103
Creation

2. Contemplating the Awe of God: The Rainbow   105

3. Contemplating the Awe of God: Seas, Walking on   107
Life's Seas

4. Contemplating the Awe of God: Controlling   109
Chaos in the Tower of Babel

5. Contemplating the Awe of God: The Virgin Birth   111

6. Contemplating the Awe of God: Multiplying   113
Bread and Fish

7. Contemplating the Awe of God: Resurrection   115
from the Dead

WEEK 8: NOT-SO-LITTLE THINGS TO LOCK UP

1. Not-So-Little Things to Lock Up: A Comment in   119
Passing

2. Not-So-Little Things to Lock Up: A Loving Touch   121

3. Not-So-Little Things to Lock Up: A Moment of   123
Your Time

4. Not-So-Little Things to Lock Up: Small Responses   125
to Crisis

5. Not-So-Little Things to Lock Up: A Word   127
of Hope

6. Not-So-Little Things to Lock Up: A Small Token   129

7. Not-So-Little Things to Lock Up: A Quick Jot   131

WEEK 9: THE TREASURED GIFT OF LISTENING

1. The Treasured Gift of Listening: To God in the   135
Quiet Moments

2. The Treasured Gift of Listening: To God in the   137
Workplace

3. The Treasured Gift of Listening: In Your Family   139
Relations

4. The Treasured Gift of Listening: In Our   141
Friendships

5. The Treasured Gift of Listening: While in Prayer 143
for Your Ministry
6. The Treasured Gift of Listening: In Your 145
Quiet Time
7. The Treasured Gift of Listening: What God 147
Always Does

WEEK 10: PRECIOUS SCENTS
1. Precious Scents: And Matters of the Heart 151
2. Precious Scents: As Sacrificial Gifts to the Christ 153
Child
3. Precious Scents: Mary's Costly, Misunderstood 155
Sacrifice
4. Precious Scents: Embalming the Living God 157
5. Precious Scents: The Sweet Fragrance of 159
Christians
6. Precious Scents: Are We Stinkers or Bloomers? 161
7. Precious Scents: Distilling and Refining Our 163
Fragrance

Acknowledgments 165
About the Author 167
Notes 169

This book is dedicated to all the people who were locked down (in one way or another) during the coronavirus pandemic that began in 2019. May you all view the carefully curated cachet of precious Bible verses contained in this book to be among the greatest treasures in your vault of valuables, no matter what circumstances you currently face.

INTRODUCTION

When state and local governments began imposing stay-at-home restrictions, no one ever dreamed of the length of time they would continue. Even as of this writing, they have worsened in scope and breadth. As our social structures and experiences in community began to shrink, I, like you, began to take stock as to what was truly valuable to me.

Some "shiny things" that once seemed so important began to lose their luster. With more time on my hands, I began to restructure how that time was spent. And the cast of characters with whom I spent it with began to shift as well. Even time itself became an unexpectedly valuable commodity. Sure, I started off making yarn pompoms and binge-watching some TV shows. But as the days toppled over one another like dominos, I began to see the momentum each one could have as it moved into the next. This was my chance to achieve some longtime goals the Lord had put on my heart regarding writing, podcasting, and live encouragement delivery.

It was in these newfound activities that I experienced an unexpected rebirth of purpose in the midst of the pandemic. I began living out a Romans 8:28 outcome that Paul explains in that famous verse: "We know that all things work together for the good of those who love God: those who are called according to His purpose." Once my purposes mirrored His more closely, I began to soar like never before, and the shiny things of this life and the people who chased after them lost their luster for me. I was able to see Him more clearly and follow Him more nearly each and every day, to loosely paraphrase an old song from the 1971 musical *Godspell*. While I can't exactly say I am grateful for COVID-19, I would be relying on little more than a flimsy foundational structure if I didn't lay everything I did moving forward in these challenging days on a divine cornerstone that is Jesus Christ.

What's in my vault looks different now. I'm making sure what is precious to me stays in lockdown and some of what I once perceived as precious is rightly discarded. I'm clinging to this vault-worthy verse from Hebrews 12:1: "Therefore, since we also have such a large cloud of witnesses surrounding us, let us lay aside every weight and the sin that so easily ensnares us."

Join me in securing what matters and discarding what doesn't as we take inventory of our sacred valuables with a fresh perspective.

WEEK 1: IN THE VAULT

IN THE VAULT: DENYING OUTSIDE ACCESS

*B*eginning in the spring of 2020, hospitals and nursing home facilities began strict protocols regarding outside visitors. Maternity wards, coronavirus areas, assisted living facilities and other caregiving homes began restricting who was permitted inside. Even the closest loved ones were often not permitted to visit mothers having babies, aged loved ones at the end of their days, or even perfectly healthy people who happened to be part of a high-risk population.

These restrictions were bitter pills to swallow, indeed. But for many of these institutions, their hands were tied. Their top priority was to ensure the safety of those entrusted to them and keep them free from the dangers of COVID, to the best of their ability. They felt their only defense was to deny outside access.

We have an obligation to deny access to the inner recesses of our hearts and minds when it comes to our spiritual life. That's why God's Word is replete with warnings about the kinds of influences from which we need to steer clear. In Leviticus 19:31, God's people are warned not to turn to mediums or seek out those who practice the occult so they will not be defiled by them.

It's also wise to restrict access to your inner circle. You may have friends who don't know the Lord that you have targeted to help discover the abundant life in Christ that you have. But take care when it comes to selecting close companions. We are told in

Proverbs 12:26 that righteous men should choose their friends carefully, since "the ways of the wicked lead them astray."

When we are surrounded with friends who share our values and our reverence for right and wrong, we are more apt to stay on a straight and narrow path. And if one or the other is tempted to diverge from that path, the friend can set them straight in a way a nonbelieving friend never could. In Proverbs 27:17 we are reminded that "iron sharpens iron, and one man sharpens another."

When we travel with like-minded companions, our posse is less vulnerable to corruption. That's why a community of believers, the "body" of Christ, is such an important part of the Christian walk this side of eternity. As the old saying goes, "we're better together."

Keys to Kingdom Living: Choose your inner circle carefully and deny access to what the Enemy may use to kill and destroy.

Doorpost: "The one who walks with the wise will become wise, but a companion of fools will suffer harm." Proverbs 13:20

IN THE VAULT: INVENTORYING YOUR VALUABLES

I remember back in the late '90s when a fire blazed near my home. Alerts began pinging continually to my phone regarding possible evacuations. My mind began to race as I thought about what I would gather up if that came to pass. Irreplaceable photographs and pets were at the top of the list. Then there was a secondary pile of silverware and jewelry. Suddenly I imagined myself without any possessions as if everything had burned down. Pets and photos—ok, those are valuable. But silver and jewelry? Those items provide no warmth or love.

The Bible is clear about what is important that remains valuable for all time: faith, hope, and love. We read about that in 1 Corinthians 13:13. But the greatest of that time-honored trifecta is love. So it follows that what we want to keep in our vault is securely centered on things above, not on earthly things, as stated in Colossians 3:2.

Sadly, our judgment alone on what belongs in the vault can be skewed or corrupted. During the pandemic, when state and local governments began imposing lockdowns and restrictions, the end was not in sight then—and as of this writing, still isn't! As our social structures and experiences in community shrank, I again began to take stock as to what was truly valuable to me. Just having a block of time became a commodity worthy of storing in my vault rather than something to be endured or even frittered away, as we all began waiting for lockdown to end.

So we began to gather. On Zoom. At "drive by" parties and tiny celebrations. And as we began to structure this kind of existence, the Lord brought new epiphanies and inspirations. And He also brought to mind a couple of other scribes once in lockdown. They faced a crossroads with much stricter treatment and literal chains and locks: Paul and John. Paul was frequently in and out of Roman jails. He wrote some of his great letters featured in the Bible while he was literally in chains. And John, who was exiled by Rome to the island of Patmos, wrote the book of Revelation based on visions he experienced while in lockdown.

God will give you some glimpses of what He wants you to know about your life and how you are spending it, too. As we sojourn through each day, we need to take stock of our fellow travelers, needed provisions, scenic turnouts, and final destinations. We would do well to come to Him humbly in prayer with an open mind and heart. In Psalm 139:23 we find David's earnest petition: "Search me God, and know my heart; test me and know my concerns." He goes on to ask God to lead him in an everlasting way (v. 24).

I'm sure we are all in agreement that the everlasting way is the only way we want to travel in this earthly journey with an eternal destination. And because time is one of the few non-renewable resources we are given in this life, we need to be good stewards of it. Indeed, God numbered our days before we were born. We should take care not to squander that gift!

I also love the verse that appears in 1 Corinthians 13:12. "For now we see indistinctly, as in a mirror, but then face to face. Now I know in part, but then I will know fully, as I am fully known." Once we meet God face to face, we will understand why His plan was always best, even when what we tried to prioritize looked different from His vision.

There's an old hymn titled "Be Thou My Vision." It's an old eighth-century hymn translated by Eleanor Hull in 1912. The hymn was inspired by an action St. Patrick took in AD 433. During the pagan feast of Beltane, the king of Ireland and the druid priests ordered all fires to be extinguished[1]. Then they would light their own huge fire from which all other fires around Ireland would be lit. But since that pagan feast coincided with Easter, St. Patrick risked his life by climbing a tall hill and lighting his own fire. He wanted to show the world that God's light shines in the darkness. When the fire could not be put out, St. Patrick was given a stage to speak to the Irish people about Jesus Christ[2]. What a testimony to trust in God's divine illumination.

Keys to Kingdom Living: Trust God's illumination as you inventory your valuables.

Doorpost: "Don't collect for yourselves treasures on earth, where moths and rust destroy and where thieves break in and steal." Matthew 6:19

IN THE VAULT: KEYS TO A SOLID, FORT-KNOX LOCKUP

When my autistic son was growing up, he frequently eloped. I learned the hard way that this meaning extended far beyond that of two people running away to get married. It also refers to individuals who bolt or run away. Because of this tendency, we had to install a variety of locks around the house. We even had to switch to a key-only front door with no handle due to his unpredictable behavior. It was a running family joke that it was sometimes harder to get out of our house than it would have been to break into it!

Our hearts and minds need to be tightly secured as well. This is so our thought life does not elope from the values and beliefs to which the deepest corners of our souls long to cling. We need to be intentional in locking out what doesn't belong in our vaults just as much as we need to secure what does.

We can start with putting off our old self, as Paul suggests in Ephesians 4:22. He reminds us of the importance of throwing off our former lives and any deceitful desires we might have. We can then allow God to put His armor onto us—the breastplate of righteousness, the shield of faith, the helmet of salvation, and the sword of truth, as we are told in Ephesians 6. We can then commit to screening what our eyes see, what our ears hear, and what our bodies do. We can ask God to help us keep intruding thoughts and behaviors at bay that run contrary to our goals and the plans and purposes God has for our lives. The importance of this lockdown is stressed in 1 Corinthians 16:9: "A wide door for effective ministry has opened for me—yet many oppose me." We need to narrow our doors to limit access from our underworld adversary who wants nothing more to intrude, distract, and destroy.

Fort Knox, also known as the United States Bullion Depository, is blessed with what is internationally known as the "gold standard" of security. Constructed in 1936, the building walls are made of nearly impenetrable granite, concrete, reinforced steel and structural steel. The roof is similarly constructed. Below-ground, the building is divided into compartments and features cryptic security procedures. Everyone who enters is provided with separate instructions on how to enter the building. All these measures are designed to protect approximately half of America's gold reserves[1].

How secure is your vault from intrusion or compromise? Is the gold God has refined in your life protected? Are you outfitted with the armor of God daily? Are you intentional about shoring yourself up from corrupting thoughts, images, and temptations from our "anything goes" world? If not, the good news is that it's never too late to shore things up. In Psalm 91 David describes the Most High God as a refuge and fortress. When we trust in Him, He will deliver us. He will faithfully shield us with His wings. And in Isaiah 54:17 we are reassured by the prophet that no weapon fashioned against us will prosper.

Join me in taking great comfort in knowing that these promises are not only vault-worthy, they are eternal!

Keys to Kingdom Living: Partner with God in the lockdown of your heart and mind.

Doorpost: "The Lord is . . . my God, my mountain where I seek refuge. My shield, the horn of my salvation, my stronghold, my refuge, and my Savior, You save me from violence." 2 Samuel 22:2–4.

IN THE VAULT: SETTING ALARMS TO DISCOURAGE INTRUSION

*A*lthough my house has several locks on doors and windows, I put little trust in the elaborate alarm systems sold today. Some feature laser motion detection systems, elaborate passwords for complex keyboard, and even fingerprint entry systems. With thefts on the rise, many people are intent on securing not only their possessions but their personal safety as well.

Of course, one of the most challenging aspects of ensuring security involves knowing when someone is trying to break into a place they are unauthorized to enter. That's where alarms come into play. Defined, an alarm in relation to security involves a warning sound or device. Some alarms are deafening, like an air horn or a high-pitched squealing sound. Others, like those found in museums and high-end jewelry stores, may be completely silent. But both alarms notify a central headquarters location or a higher authority that a break-in is underway.

In our spiritual life, we are often unaware of how often and to what degree the Enemy is attempting to break in and steal our valuables. His "flaming arrows," described in Ephesians 6:16, are continual. And the stakes of the Enemy's war continually waged against us are quite high. In 1 Peter 5:8, our evil adversary is compared to a roaring lion prowling about and desiring to devour and tear us to pieces.

There are a couple of ways we can recognize the sound of the alarm when it comes to breaches of the vault of our hearts and minds. One way is to recognize when we are confused about a voice that suggests doing something which is out of line with God's Word. We can know for sure that God never leads us to do anything that runs contrary to His laws. In Numbers 23:19 we read, "God is not a man who lies, or a son of man who changes his mind. Does He speak and not act, or promise and not fulfill?" The answer? Never.

Another way is to stay focused on the sound of the Gatekeeper so imposters are easily recognized. God's Word clearly identifies some ways we can know our Gatekeeper. One way involves blocking out the voices of others and sometimes not even trusting what we think we see. In John 10:3–5 we read that the doorkeeper opens the gate for the sheep and that "the sheep hear his voice. He calls out his own sheep by name and leads them out. When he has brought all his own outside, he goes ahead of them. The sheep follow him because they recognize his voice. They will never follow a stranger; instead, they will run away from him." Jesus provided these examples to help us know the importance of recognizing who we are to follow and who we are to avoid at all costs. Steering clear of trouble involves heeding an alarm of caution.

One of the most important things we need to know about alarms is that the person they protect must be intentional in not just heeding them but setting them. We need to ask God to give us discernment to help us recognize when the spiritual valuables we want to secure are under threat of being compromised or obliterated altogether. We can also surround ourselves with like-minded companions.

Recently, my older son was considering something that conflicted with his values. I weighed in with my two cents, but because he is an adult child my advice only went so far. Another friend with solid core values pointed out the conflict of the action he was considering with the values he knew my son uphold. This reminder helped my son take stock of what mattered most—what lined up with God's Word—and he backpedaled to his original position and embraced the integrity he nearly lost. Thankfully, he heard that second alarm loud and clear. It's my hope and prayer that all of us will heed the alarms and avoid potential loss and heartache.

Keys to Kingdom Living: Take care not only to set alarms to guard what matters most but to respond to breaches of security before the loss is too great.

Doorpost: "My son, keep your father's command, and don't reject your mother's teaching. Always bind them to your heart; tie them around your neck." Proverbs 6:20–21

IN THE VAULT: BOLSTERING YOUR SECURITY

On July 9, 1982, a thirty-four-year-old painter and decorator named Michael Fagan climbed over the railing near the gates of one of the entrances and entered Buckingham Palace[1]. According to Scotland Yard, he then freely moved through the palace corridors for approximately thirty minutes until he arrived inside Queen Elizabeth's bedroom. Though an alarm had been tripped in the proximity of King George V's valuable stamp collection, it was dismissed as false.

But there were other cracks in the system. The night patrolmen had just gone off-duty. The footman was out walking the dogs. One of the on-duty maids was cleaning in a room near the queen, but the door was closed. And two phone calls made by Queen Elizabeth to the palace telephone operator failed to bring help. We'll never know if these negligent staffers were sacked or not, but Fagan was arrested for trespassing at the palace.

Is the palace where your vaulted spiritual treasures are stored secure? Or could Satan easily get a foothold?

There are ways to shore up potential cracks in your security system. One way is to make sure you thoroughly understand what God's Word requires of us. In Micah 6:8 we read that He has told us what is good and what the Lord requires of us. We are to act justly, to love faithfulness, and to walk humbly with our God. When we honor God's ten commandments and study His Word to fully unpack what it means to follow Him, we are securing our foundation against compromise. Understanding more about Satan's schemes can help disrupt this protocol to some degree, even if those insights don't entirely stop the Enemy dead in his tracks. He wants nothing more than to try to come between the godly life we want to lead and the life we may be tempted to lead. We are told this in 1 Thessalonians 5:6: "So then, we must not sleep, like the rest, but we must stay awake and be serious."

You might be tempted to chuckle as you read such a seemingly obvious verse. But we would all do well to implement the wisdom found there. The English footman, maid, operator, and patrolmen undoubtedly paid some sort of price for their complacency. The same is true for us. Ask God to show you where you can shore up your security so you can make sure your vault remains secure.

Keys to Kingdom Living: Review your security continually, looking for potential areas of vulnerability, and shore them up with God's help.

Doorpost: "Therefore, be alert, since you don't know what day your Lord is coming. But know this: if the homeowner had known what time the thief was coming, he would have stayed alert and not let his house be broken into." Matthew 24:42–43

IN THE VAULT: SURVIVING ATTACKS

*I*n his first job, my husband was employed as an engineer with an American electronics company that had several contracts with government defense entities. My husband and those who worked with him had to obtain top security clearance. Their part of the building was inaccessible to anyone without this clearance, and music was piped in every day to prevent conversations from being taped or recorded in any way.

One day, one of his fellow employees failed to show up for work. Eventually, someone from the company contacted the apartment building at the address provided only to find the apartment completely empty and no traces of the guy whatsoever.

He turned out to be a spy. And the damage he had done was more untraceable than the significant steps he'd taken to gain entry. Despite great measures on the part of the company, its security had been compromised.

This can happen in our own lives, too. Sometimes, Satan can get a foothold. He can infiltrate a weak area and wreak havoc. If we are fortunate and diligent enough to recognize it, we can mitigate the damage. We can implement these three key steps.

Step 1: We can be open to admitting vulnerabilities and be accountable. God already knows where we have neglected to shore up a crack or fissure. We must be accountable to Him for our part in any security breach. Partner with Him in this process. Ask Him to reveal anything you may be unaware of that contributed to the breach and for Him to help you learn from it. David modeled this beautifully in Psalm 139:23 when he asks God to search his heart and test him and his anxious thoughts so that he might be led into a posture of repentance and forgiveness.

Step 2: Repent and ask for forgiveness. Once we have identified our wrongdoings, we are in position to repent and ask God for His forgiveness. Fortunately, we never have to wonder whether God will forgive us or hold a grudge. He promises that "as far as the east is from the west," that's how far has he removed our sin from us (Psalm 103:12). What a blessing to know that the perfect Almighty God offers more grace than some of our imperfect friends, even though He meets every high standard Himself!

Step 3: Pray for limited levels of loss and restoration. Once we have been forgiven and sanctified, that doesn't mean that we won't face some consequences for our sin. We can ask God in transparent prayer and petition to limit the impact of what we've done with regard to our own life as well as the lives of others. Like any prayer, we should pray this kind of petition with a humble heart. We should understand and accept that the answer will rest perfectly within the framework of God's will, even if we experience some pain in that answer. Thankfully, we can know and trust that God will use what we learn for our benefit and undoubtedly for His glory.

Keys to Kingdom Living: Work at identifying vulnerabilities and ask God to help you mitigate the damage and extent of theft and loss.

Doorpost: "All scripture is God-breathed and useful for teaching, rebuking, correcting and training in righteousness so that the servant of God may be equipped for every good work." 2 Timothy 3:16–17

IN THE VAULT: THANKING GOD FOR
HIS PROTECTION

*J*n the 1993 movie *Dave*, a scenario of bravery and self-sacrifice plays out like the stuff of, well, Hollywood. In the film, a Secret Service agent assigned to the US president is charged with the guarding an impersonating president. It's part of an elaborate ruse orchestrated by the ailing president's existing cabinet members to preserve the status quo.

The fraudulent scheme is eventually dismantled. Ving Rhames's character, bodyguard Duane Stevenson, then confesses to the impersonator Dave Kovic, played by Kevin Klein, that he would have been willing to take a bullet for Kovic even though he was not, in fact, the president. Now that's dedication!

Before your mind skips to fast-forward and you think there might not be anyone you know willing to do the same for you, let me assure you that you're wrong.

Jesus Christ came to Earth leaving behind all His glory to be born in a manger. He endured ridicule and humiliation from doubters, church leaders, and government officials. He took a couple of nails and hours of excruciation hanging on the cross for you and the rest of mankind to secure a home in heaven for you. Until He comes again in glory, He continues to keep His promises. Our names are written in the Book of Life when we put our faith and trust in Him. And, regardless of what is happening to us in your current circumstances, we can depend on God as He alone maintains the long view.

David writes eloquently about God's protection. In Psalm 91:1–6 he describes God as his refuge and fortress, expressing gratitude for the hedge of protection enjoyed under the shadow of His covering wings. He cites God's faithfulness as a shield and buckler. And in Psalm 27:5 David speaks of being hidden in the shelter of God the Father in the day of trouble.

Paul, in Romans 8:38–39, puts it even more fervently: "For I am persuaded that not even death or life, angels or rulers, things present or things to come, hostile powers, height or depth, or any other created thing will have the power to separate us from the love of God that is in Christ Jesus our Lord!"

What a blessing it is to know that we can take these assurances and promises to the bank! They are far and away the greatest treasures we can possess when we put our faith and trust in Him. We are reminded in Hebrews 13:8 that Jesus Christ is the same yesterday, today, and forever. In a world that is continually changing—and not for the better—that is good news indeed.

Keys to Kingdom Living: We can trust God to redirect us, and we can thank Him for the restoration He does in our lives on this side of eternity and beyond.

Doorpost: "I know the One I have believed in and am persuaded that He is able to guard what has been entrusted to me until that day. Hold on to the pattern of sound teaching that you have heard from me, in the faith and love that are in Christ Jesus. Guard, through the Holy Spirit who lives in us, that good thing entrusted to you." 2 Timothy 1:12–14

WEEK 2: LAND WORTH SECURING

LAND WORTH SECURING: EDEN AND ITS PERFECTION

I remember the first time I saw someone playing the game blackjack in a movie. As you may know, the object of the game is to get the cards you are dealt as close as you can to the sum of twenty-one without going over the number. The opponent who gets closest without going over wins the hand. Like any competition with stakes, the process can be nerve-wracking. Games of stakes and unpredictable odds unnerve me. The cost of losing outweighs the risk for me. I prefer the status quo and a predictable order to things.

Our God of divine order established just such an environment when He created His magnificent heavens and the earth. The world He created featured abundant provision, unimaginable beauty, harmony between man and animals, serene security, and a setting void of work demands. Adam, and eventually Eve, lived in perfect peace and abundance so unimaginable to us today. They never had to stress out about what to wear when they lived in God's garden. They had no need for shelter from harsh elements or any need to beautify themselves or their surroundings. Yet in a single moment, both of them went from eternal serenity to utter tragedy and chaos.

Though the Bible doesn't say, I would imagine the single biggest problem the two of them had after they were banished from the Garden of Eden was regret. From time to time, we must all regret the bad choices we have made and how it may have impacted our lives and those of our loved ones. But the sin of Adam and Eve not only took down everyone who's ever lived, it forever removed them from the idyllic existence they once had the privilege of enjoying and separated them from the Entity who created them and the One who loved them the most.

We don't have any experience with a loss of perfect living as Adam and Eve did, but we still struggle with our quest to achieve it. We want ideal figures, perpetually youthful appearances, perfectly manicured lawns, and impeccably decorated homes. We want our children to behave perfectly, to achieve perfectly, and to avoid making mistakes as they shoot their way to the top of their respective fields. We want idyllic relationships devoid of conflict and strife, redolent with romance, and brimming with familial love reminiscent of a *Little House on the Prairie* episode.

God isn't the one filling our minds with these unrealistic expectations. That's Satan's specialty. He wants to do what He can to discourage you, rendering you ineffective in your own life and in the lives of others. Don't let him distract you. Keep your mind rooted in reality, and keep your heart and mind focused on the fact that someday we will be restored to perfection and bask in its unmatched beauty for all eternity.

Keys to Kingdom Living: Let go of lofty expectations and their resulting frustrations.

Doorpost: "You were the seal of perfection, full of wisdom and perfect in beauty. You were in Eden, the garden of God." Ezekiel 28:12–13

LAND WORTH SECURING: EDEN UNDONE

I have a morbid curiosity about Earth's comeuppance. Movies depicting the end of the world fascinate me. There's an inherent sense of justice, seeing mankind face a world run amok after years of neglect and abuse, at all our own hands. Man's development of infrastructure has taken a toll on the world over the centuries. This planet is a far cry from what God created.

I can't help thinking of the Bible verse which says, "God is not mocked" (Galatians 6:7). Modern-day fracking, offshore drilling, and a ransacking of natural resources have all wreaked havoc with our terra firma since the garden of Eden fell victim to sin. It would be very hard to argue against the notion that the environment is engaged in a downward spiral of deterioration, even if it hasn't reached a Hollywood ending yet. As Satan has a foothold in this imperfect world, God is patiently waiting for as many of His people as possible to come to repentance before He obliterates Earth to usher in the New Jerusalem. Thankfully, we don't need to be alarmed about the final outcome because as Christians we are heirs to this long-promised kingdom.

Unlike the dramas of Hollywood that must play out in a small finite time frame, the actual, ultimate demise of our planet may continue to be more gradual. The deterioration of God's creation occurred in shifts. Once Adam and Eve were banished from the garden of Eden, as recorded in Genesis 3:24, any remnant of perfection was totally off-limits. In its time, the garden was even guarded so as to prevent anyone from reentering. Subsequently, Earth endured floods, including the flood that Noah experienced that reshaped the continents of our planet. Our planet has faced droughts, famines, pestilence, earthquakes, scorching heat, bitter cold, debilitating disease, and a host of mankind's crimes against humanity.

As our eyes take in images of disasters and our hearts fill with sorrow over their repercussions, we as Christians can know and trust in God's perfect plan. Despite the deterioration of our world as we know it, He has secured our destiny. If we feel fear coming on, we can remember that He promises He will never leave us or forsake us (Deuteronomy 31:6). We can exchange the pages of negative newspaper headlines with the pages in our Bibles filled with God's promises, along with examples of His limitless faithfulness to generations who've loved and trusted in Him and His promises.

Even as I am writing this, a friend is stranded in her house, surrounded by water. All the bordering streets are flooded. She is fighting anxiety, trusting in God, and praying for safety and security. In the face of news reports and the history of flooding in her area, she knows that nothing can separate her from God, as He has promised in Romans 8:38–39.

It's tempting to view the future with pessimism. We can accept the reality of what is happening around us, pray for God's will in all matters, and still thank Him that although the Eden of old is long gone, His perfection will return when He makes all things new, as promised in Revelation 21:5. May we always hold fast to that eternal perspective.

Keys to Kingdom Living: Look not at the world but at God and His promises.

Doorpost: "The Angel of the LORD encamps around those who fear Him, and rescues them." Psalm 34:7

LAND WORTH SECURING: TERRAIN FROM EGYPT TO EXODUS

*W*hen I was a kid, my parents would pack my brother and me in the station wagon for family vacations. It always started out amiably enough, but the inevitable "space wars" would eventually begin. My brother was often banished to what he called "the cage," the back hatch of the wagon at a time when seat belts were options as opposed to mandates. But if we were both seated in the back seat, he was relegated to the right and I was relegated to the left, leaving the small space between designated as no-man's-land. This buffer was intended to keep the peace.

When the Israelites began their exodus from Egypt, they initially traveled through a kind of no-man's-land as well. Moses led them to the outskirts of Egyptian civilization, but they remained a good distance from the land God promised them. We read in Exodus 13 of their obedience to head toward the Red Sea and even cross miraculously through it, unharmed.

When we trust in God to lead us where He wants us to go, we enjoy a no-man's-land level of protection. No matter what circumstance we face, God promises in His Word over and over that He has our back. In Romans 8:38, Paul writes of his conviction that death, any hostile powers that be, or what happens today or tomorrow can't separate us from God's love.

This kind of faith that frequently flies in the face of logic is the hallmark of a Christ follower. So often God leads us into what seem like impossible situations where our very safety and even our lives appear to be threatened by a task or mission we may undertake for Him. There are two possible outcomes to these situations. We can be saved from the temporal destruction of, say, the Red Sea, the belly of a whale, the mouth of a lion, or the flames of the fiery furnace. But it's important to distinguish God's will as well as His ability in every circumstance. In Daniel 3, we read the declaration of Shadrach, Meshach, and Abednego, that even if they were thrown into the furnace, they knew God was *able* to deliver them. But they added that *even if He did not*—meaning they would perish—they still were not willing to bow down to another god.

There are other heroes of the Bible who faced similar situations and became martyrs for their choice to stand up for God rather than men. John the Baptist, Stephen, Peter, James, and a host of others who have—and will—come after them, sacrificed their earthly lives for their eternal beliefs. Though long gone, they didn't tarry in no-man's-land. They crossed over into paradise, where they await the day Jesus will come again in glory and establish the New Jerusalem.

You may have crossed your share of no-man's-land territories in your life. Or you may even be headed into one now. Though you don't know how it will turn out, if you belong to Jesus, you can rest assured it will not be your final destination.

Keys to Kingdom Living: We are sojourners in this land but heirs of the next.

Doorpost: "For we do not have an enduring city here; instead, we seek the one to come." Hebrews 13:14

LAND WORTH SECURING: THE WILDERNESS

The open space behind the house I lived in as a teenager stretched endlessly, as far as my eyes could see. As a young writer grappling with adolescent growing pains, I would often set out in my boots with a notepad and pen to brave tall grass as I made my way to a small clearing where I would journal and write poetry. The music of the cicadas and the babbling brook played just below my favorite rocky perch. It struck me then how much easier it was to surround myself with inspiration and thought in the middle of nowhere than it was to court the muse in my own room. The need to leave familiarity behind to encounter new thoughts and ideas is as well-worn as the notion of penning our innermost thoughts.

My self-imposed time in the wilderness was relegated to an hour or so, a sharp contrast to the sentences imposed on the characters in the Bible. The children of Israel wandered forty years in their wilderness. King Nebuchadnezzar wandered for seven years in the wilderness. It's recorded in Luke that John the Baptist spent most of his life ministering about Jesus in the Judean wilderness. Jesus Himself entered the wilderness where He was tempted by Satan, only to emerge victoriously after resisting temptations.

Today when people hear the term "wilderness," they think of a place where hard-core campers might go to get away from civilization to boast about their ability to conquer whatever nature throws at them, only to re-enter society as conquerors of sorts. But the wilderness we read about in the Bible is more than just open and desolate space. It is a remote, seemingly lifeless place that is almost God-forsaken in its appearance and nature. It is in barren and desolate places where we are most likely to come to the end of ourselves. We are free from distractions and diversions, alone with our thoughts. And, if we have the presence of mind, we have an opportunity to connect with our Creator in a profound way. But the wilderness can also represent the barren place where men and women reside when they are not in communion with God.

The Israelites did not make a beeline for the promised land. God is the one who led that pilgrimage. Unlike modern navigational tools that plot the most efficient course from *A* to *B*, God's agenda is more about the journey than the destination. Refinement was God's primary goal in relegating the Israelites to decades of trudging through the sand. He wanted His people to be fully reliant on Him, from the manna they ate in the morning to the quail He would send in the evening. He would summon water from rocks.

In our own lives, when we find ourselves in a wilderness, we might be inclined to engage our own GPS, but what God really wants us to do is follow His leading and let Him illuminate our next steps. Join me in trusting God's itinerary for your life.

Keys to Kingdom Living: It's only when we lose ourselves that God's agenda for our lives can truly rule and reign in our hearts, our minds, and our very lives.

Doorpost: "Prepare the way of the LORD in the wilderness; make a straight highway for our God in the desert." Isaiah 40:3

LAND WORTH SECURING: INHABITING EARTH'S PROMISED LAND

*O*n one of my trips to Europe, I was in the throes of jet lag. I was trying to push through the afternoon to try to get some things done. Suddenly, it became clear to me that I needed to return to my room and rest. I literally couldn't find my way back to the hotel—I was so exhausted that I had to activate the navigation system on my phone. I literally wandered about, utterly lost.

The Jewish refugees from Egypt felt much the same way. After forty years of wandering through the Sinai desert and years of battles under the leadership of Joshua, they were finally able to enter the land God promised them. Imagine the feeling of finally possessing what was promised to you and the generations before you. Imagine finally setting foot on that very land and claiming it.

If you didn't already know what happened next, you might imagine a perfectly harmonious environment. Unfortunately, the promised land was inhabited by imperfect people and remained a target of foreign opposition by still more imperfect people. (The length of this historic time period, referred to as the time of the judges, is disputed; the chronology is, by many, believed to be the 410 years between the death of Joshua and the establishment of the monarchy.)

An idyllic promised land for the Jewish people remains as elusive as the grapes do to the proverbial fox from Aesop's famous fable. Both simply cannot reach that lofty vine. Throughout history, the Jews have possessed the land of their holy nation only to have it conquered again and again. The disputed territory remains the focus of tribal wars, bloody infighting, and so-called holy wars to this day and will continue until the day Jesus comes again in glory.

The only everlasting royal priesthood and holy nation is still to come. But we can enjoy some of the fruits of God's promises in the lands we currently inhabit. I view a promised land on earth in this way: we are enjoying God's promises in our daily life. We nurture a perspective of banking on a life to come. Our feet are firmly planted on terra firma, but we remain mindful that we are "not of this world," as Jesus says in John 8:36. And within this mindset we enjoy beauty and purpose in light of all God has done, and we look forward to what He will do. We enjoy His creation, find fulfillment in expanding His flock, and love others deeply from the heart.

One example of a promised land scenario here on earth may involve betrothal, marriage, and sex. When Christians who have saved their purity for marriage are engaged, they continue to wait until their wedding day arrives to consummate their marriage. They still enjoy each other's company, bask in their love for one another, and even dream of and imagine what will one day come to pass. They anticipate this, even though they don't cross over to the actual experience until the very day their promise comes to pass and the two become one flesh.

Keys to Kingdom Living: Promised land living involves a mindset, not merely a real estate parcel.

Doorpost: "The LORD your God will give you rest, and He will give you this land." Joshua 1:13

LAND WORTH SECURING: THE
COMMISSION TO DISTANT LANDS

*I*remember the first time I saw quicksand in a B-rate black-and-white movie. Some poor explorer on an African expedition fell into a pool of the murky substance that swallowed him up in about fifteen seconds. Terrified, I immediately asked my mother about quicksand and whether I needed to worry about it in everyday life.

My girlish terror over what might be encountered in African jungles subsided and was replaced by first-hand knowledge of the beauty and peace I know can be found in the villages where missionaries have transformed tribal infighting into communities rich in brotherly love. That's what happens when God gets ahold of a heart open to His leadings. I remember the first ordinary person I knew well whom God tapped for international missions. She told me her husband suddenly felt a passion for the people of Africa and their plight of economic and spiritual poverty. He told her he wanted to go to Niger, and I remember her saying, "I can tell you right now, I'm not going." Since that time, my friend and her husband have built an orphanage, trained leaders, and led Bible studies for thousands of people as they've spent months on end traveling through Africa to fulfill God's commission on their lives.

Because that kind of sacrificial joy—and the eternal investment that results—is inevitably contagious, it wasn't long before I found myself going to meetings about short-term African mission trips. There is something exhilarating about saying yes to Jesus's Great Commission. In Matthew 28:19, Jesus says to "go, therefore, and make disciples of all nations, baptizing them in the name of the Father and of the Son and of the Holy Spirit." Just knowing I have responded to that call for all nations excites me greatly. Because I moved past my fears, more names may be added to the Book of Life. Thanks in part to my Spirit-led response, seeds there continue to be reinvested in all kinds of new ways, even today.

The most useful thing I've learned about mission work involves the many ways Christians like me can participate. We can penetrate distant lands with God's love and message of salvation in numerous ways that don't involve living in those countries full-time. When we sponsor a child overseas and invest in their life, we are making disciples. When we provide financial stipends to international mission efforts, we are helping fulfill the Great Commission. We can build relationships and offer words of encouragement via social media to our brothers and sisters overseas. With our continual outreach of love and messages of hope, we can foster discipleship with them. This is one of the hallmarks of the information age in which we live: Christians can impact distant lands from the privacy of their own homes.

However, if you are healthy enough, you might pray to be filled with courage and strength from God to tie your bandana to your walking stick and ready your passport for adventure. Don't hesitate to say yes to God. You won't be sorry!

Keys to Kingdom Living: Your divine passport is ready for stamping when you are ready to journey forward in obedience.

Doorpost: "For I will take you from the nations and gather you from all the countries, and will bring you into your own land. I will also sprinkle clean water on you. . . . I will remove your heart of stone and give you a heart of flesh." Ezekiel 36:24–26

LAND WORTH SECURING: THE
ULTIMATE PROMISED LAND

*B*lame old cartoons for the flowing white robe, harp, and cloud-seat that popular culture has associated with heavenly dwelling. Whenever a cartoon character would die, soft and soothing harp music would play in the background as these stereotypical props would appear.

We read nowhere in the Bible of this sort of scenario. Fortunately, in this day and age, we are blessed to live at a time when Christian writers are eager to take up the topic of what heaven will be like. Gifted authors like Randy Alcorn are making important inroads in unraveling what remains at best a mystery and at worst an obstacle that challenges our contemporary world views mired in Western thought and in the limitations of our humanity.

Less effective, and decidedly less accurate, are the depictions of heaven put forth in films and television shows. Even so, the idea of eating whatever we want to our heart's content, as depicted in the 1991 film *Defending Your Life*, certainly holds some appeal . . . but I digress. Some films and books of late feature people who claim to have died and then been resuscitated, revealing some of the things they have seen and heard. I will not debate the validity of those stories in these pages.

The important things to know about heaven lie in what we can expect when we get there and the hard fact that those who belong to God are 100 percent guaranteed to arrive at their destination. Jesus Himself promised that He was spearheading this eternal effort. "In My Father's house are many dwelling places; if not, I would have told you. I am going away to prepare a place for you." Jesus said this in John 14:2. Jesus assures us there will be plenty of room for His beloved children and that He Himself will be making the preparations! Imagine a luxurious hotel setting. Perhaps there's a card with your name on it, welcoming you, or a chocolate on your pillow, or other personal touches that make you feel special or important. We can't in our wildest dreams imagine the eternal riches we are poised to inherit.

We receive insightful glimpses of heaven's specifications in Revelation 21 and 22. The overall picture is that of a bride adorned for her husband. Our God is well-versed in divine order; everything will be an unprecedented delight to all our senses. We'll feast our eyes on the finest building materials, and we will inhale heady heavenly aromas. In 2 Corinthians 2:15, we read of the "fragrance of Christ." (This will bear sharp contrast to our perpetual earthly battles with body odor and kitchen stench.)

Fine wine may be part of the aromas and tasty flavors to be enjoyed in eternity. Jesus says in Mark 14:25 that He will drink "the fruit of the vine" with His people in heaven. In Revelation 22 we read of the Tree of Life, so some assume there will be fab fruit in heaven.

We read what *isn't* in heaven, too—no more crying, pain, darkness, or wickedness. What could be more heavenly than that!

Keys to Kingdom Living: Prepare your heart and senses to be dazzled by eternity.

Doorpost: "But as it is written: What eye did not see and ear did not hear, and what never entered the human mind—God prepared this for those who love Him." 1 Corinthians 2:9

WEEK 3: THE INVESTMENT OF SPIRITUAL TRAINING

THE INVESTMENT OF SPIRITUAL
TRAINING: TRAINING FOR GOD

ard-bodied spend countless hours a week sculpting their bodies into lean, lithe physiques. We curl free weights for ripped biceps, run miles to cultivate endurance, and press on with pushups to build our strength. But what kind of time are we putting in to run "the race that lies before us," as Paul writes in Hebrews 12:1?

For some, the Bible is like a dust-covered exercise machine shoved in an unused corner of a room. Or maybe the leaflet you receive at church to write down answers, reflections, and goals is like the keychain exercise tag that's rarely swiped at the gym door you neglect to darken. In this day and age, with web and podcast church services, there is less of an excuse to miss keeping the Sabbath day holy, but as with the exercise we try to avoid, excuses do just that. They leap up like kernels of popcorn, and before you know it, those excuses outnumber the kernels of intention.

All of us can probably relate to areas in our life where the term "spiritual couch potato" applies. Our spiritual nature will likely remain sedentary unless we implement strategies for action. It's up to us to be proactive in developing its full potential. By taking this aspect of personal growth seriously, we are sowing seeds for our own growth with heavenly guidance to help us reach our full potential. And we can partner with God in that gardening effort to help others, including those around us—our friends, family, and those within our sphere of influence.

Jesus modeled several areas where we need "personal training." We need to meet alone with God every day, as He did. Just as a trainer looks over your body to see which areas need work, so will God look into your heart and, if you are listening, He will point out those pesky "work needed" areas. And just as He also carefully selected a group of men to be His disciples, we must also surround ourselves with like-minded souls who want to accompany us on our journey.

Finally, we need to continually give thanks to God and praise Him for all He has done, is doing, and will continue to do in our lives. Jesus included prayers of thanksgiving when breaking bread. But He even offered them up as He prayed and suffered at Gethsemane. He glorified God as He prayed in adoration, "*Abba,* Father! All things are possible for You*" (Mark 14:36). We build our gratitude muscles the more we thank God for His continued faithfulness in our lives.

As we seek God's perspective on large and small goals, we can evaluate our progress. As we ask the Holy Spirit to identify areas of weakness where more work, attention, and commitment may be needed, we prepare for the race God has marked out for us by wholly dedicating ourselves to Him. It should never be considered as a sign of failure when we identify the need to rededicate or refocus in this manner. Rather it's an opportunity to draw closer to Him. Moving closer to Him is, after all, the goal of every heart who earnestly seeks after God.

Keys to Kingdom Living: Spiritual fitness must be fiercely pursued for us to achieve it successfully on any level.

Doorpost: "Therefore, brothers [and sisters], by the mercies of God, I urge you to present your bodies as a living sacrifice, holy and pleasing to God; this is your spiritual worship." Romans 12:1

THE INVESTMENT OF SPIRITUAL TRAINING: THE PRINCIPLE OF SPECIFICITY

*F*itness training is generally based on six primary concepts. Each has a spiritual application as well. We won't naturally develop into an effective soldier in the army of God without implementing a real intent to continually improve and grow.

The first of the six concepts, the principle of *specificity*, states that what you train for is what you achieve. So if strength is your physical goal, a fitness trainer can structure specific exercises designed to accomplish this goal. The same principal can apply to goal-setting in our spiritual life if we take the time and effort to identify and pursue it.

But, like gym-goers, there are those who pursue and those who procrastinate. How often have we gone to church and heard a great sermon about change or challenge, only to stuff our response paper in a drawer or, worse yet, the circular file? The best way to kick off the specificity process is to devote a specific quiet time to sit before the Lord and dedicate it to this purpose. You may need to dedicate more than one quiet time for this specific purpose. As you sit and ask Him to show you what needs work in your life, jot down what He brings to mind. This spiritual look in the mirror, with God's help, can launch our transformation.

As you write down what God reveals, think of specific people or situations that make this area challenging for you. Then examine the areas of weakness and think about your desired result. For instance, if you find you are discontented, you will want to practice more gratitude in your life. A good next step would be to use a Bible with a concordance or a web search engine to look for Bible verses that include words like "thanksgiving" and "grateful." Write these verses down and keep them in a handy place for daily meditation and reflection. You might want to download praise songs with the same theme to further reinforce the verses.

Another helpful way of practicing specificity training and organizing your thoughts is to keep a journal. If you are crafty, you might include drawings or pictures of people or things you are grateful for, like family, friends, or your grandfather's Bible. Copies of your goals and the appropriate verses could also be included, along with any thoughts related to your progress. You might include notes about occasional missteps and pledges to press on with God's help. But the overall purpose of such documentation is to encourage, so don't get bogged down in lamenting all the ways you fall short.

If you're reading this and thinking that journaling feels like a daunting task, pray to God to give you the discipline to see specificity through, starting with small increments. The rewards will far outweigh the sacrifices.

᛭

Keys to Kingdom Living: Exercising our spiritual habits enhances our effectiveness as difference-making Christians.

Doorpost: "You will seek Me and find Me when you search for Me with all your heart." Jeremiah 29:13

THE INVESTMENT OF SPIRITUAL
TRAINING: THE PRINCIPLE OF
OVERLOAD

*I*n 2015, fifteen-year-old CJ Cummings made history as not only the strongest boy but as the strongest man in his weight class.[1] Lifting 386 pounds over his head in his third and final "clean and jerk" attempt at the USA Weightlifting Championship in Dallas, announcer Jonas Westbrook reported that it appeared as though he was "lifting feathers"![2]

But Cummings didn't start his lifting career with that heavy load. He worked for years and years, pushing himself hard daily. This is called the principle of *overload*: training a part of the body above the level to which it's accustomed. We can't expect total recall of every Bible verse that means something to us after we memorize our first one. Being a Christ-follower and an avid student of the Bible requires years of thoughtful study and attention to life application day in and day out. We can't transition into spending zero quiet time with God to devoting hours on end of uninterrupted time and expect ourselves to be fully present.

Just as an endurance runner trains with short sprints and works their way up to a 10K, so can you structure your goals to push yourself a little more each day, each month, each year. If your goal involves an increase in tithing, don't impulsively empty out your entire bank account. Pray about an amount that God has in mind to stretch your giving. Or if you want to meet with God every morning, start with five minutes and work your way up to a time allotment that feels comfortable and rewarding. Perhaps you want to improve your disposition and interactions with your family members. Instead of just flatly telling yourself to be nice every moment, set a goal of saying one encouraging thing to each of your family members daily, and build from there.

By setting small, achievable goals, you will experience success and you'll also be encouraged to build on that foundation in the coming weeks. Although you may be thinking that you should focus on only one area at a time to improve, ask God to help you "come up higher" in all the areas He wants to work on in your life. As He promises in Philippians 1:6, "He who started a good work in you will carry it on to completion until the day of Christ Jesus." Of course, all His good works will not be completed until that day. But between now and then, we still need to keep seeking His help as He works in our lives to help us grow and be better disciplined.

Obstacles will appear alongside the principle of overload in your goal-setting. But one aspect of this principle won't apply to the spiritual application: If you pray for help with change and growth and follow God's lead in your life, you won't feel over-loaded but instead will feel strengthened by pressing toward spiri-tual practices tweaked for His glory.

Keys to Kingdom Living: Count on God for balance.

Doorpost: "A lazy man doesn't roast his game, but to a diligent man, his wealth is precious." Proverbs 12:27

THE INVESTMENT OF SPIRITUAL TRAINING: THE PRINCIPLE OF PROGRESSION

*I*n training, the principle of *progression* states that it's essential to move on to the next level of weights or cardio once you have mastered your current undertaking. It is the key to avoid getting temporarily or permanently stuck. For many years, my schedule dictated that I arrive at the gym at 5:45 a.m. along with an infinitely more interesting cast of characters. All were serious about exercise, but some were more successful than others.

One guy's actions, in particular, caught my eye each time I saw him down on the exercise mat. He would wield his arms and legs in a variety of positions not akin to yoga or Tai Chi or any other recognizable fitness discipline. Day in, day out, he did the same thing. I finally asked one of the personal trainers one day what his exercises were designed to accomplish, and he replied, to the best of his knowledge, absolutely nothing, beyond amusing the staff.

It's very true that in anything we begin, if we don't know what we are doing, we are simply spinning our wheels. Given the fact that life is demanding and our time is already crunched, it's a shame to let such frittering away come to pass. So when it comes to spiritual disciplines, it's important we build on our groundwork by asking God for discernment about raising, or at least changing, our goals regularly.

A good starting point for the principle of progression in our spiritual life is to map out stretching goals. Perhaps you enjoy visiting other places of worship when you travel. Or you might want to expand your exposure to other worship venues locally, as opportunity permits. And if a variety of worship experiences are available at your home church, think about trying one out just to shake up your routine. Or maybe you can explore a new area of ministry. These kinds of changes are important for the mature Christians who find themselves in a spiritual rut.

Someone I know was stuck in spiritual quicksand. He described how he and his wife felt called to leave their church home and help with a church plant—the birth of a new church— a few miles away. The experience reinvigorated them, much to their delight and surprise. The gentleman and his wife found themselves making new young friends. They were in a position to share their wisdom, while the young people shared their contagious joy, boundless energy, and hunger for their wisdom and encouragement.

The change brought them another unexpected blessing. Because the new church was close to their residence, they were able to ride their bikes as opposed to driving a long distance. This took their previous wheel-spinning full circle and enabled them to lose unwanted pounds. We don't want to spin our wheels for God, but instead we want to be effective hands and feet for Him. By regularly upping our game, we are able increase our effectiveness and joy.

Keys to Kingdom Living: Remix and reinvigorate your spiritual disciplines regularly, while permitting yourself a measure of freedom to change things up for yourself now and then.

Doorpost: "For the turning away of the inexperienced will kill them, and the complacency of fools will destroy them." Proverbs 1:32

THE INVESTMENT OF SPIRITUAL TRAINING: THE PRINCIPLE OF ACCOMMODATION

*W*hen athletes fail to make changes to their workouts, their bodies begin to atrophy. An athlete in this predicament cannot be guaranteed peak performance moving forward. In order to counteract this principle of *accommodation*, their trainers engage a twofold approach. This approach combines the implementation of quantitative measures and qualitative measures. The qualitative aspect involves changing loads—for instance, increasing an amount of weight being lifted. The quantitative approach involves replacing exercises altogether.

In our Christian walk, we have to be careful we don't throw the baby out with the bathwater. In order to serve God in our highest capacity, we need to double-check our motives and our call to service on a regular basis. Are we teaching Sunday school only because we enjoy being around the little kids, or do we really feel called to impart biblical truths to the next generation? Has that zeal that was once present in our teaching grown passionless and stale after years and years of doing it, even as we cannot imagine our lives without that structure?

Change is indeed harder as we age, but one thing that never changes is God's desire for us to love and serve Him at 100 percent capacity. We are told in Luke 10 to love the Lord our God with all our heart, soul, strength, and mind, and love our neighbor as ourself. If we answer the call of loving our neighbor as ourselves, we commit to giving them 100 percent of ourselves as we serve both God and man.

When a friend is pouring her heart out and our mind starts drifting to our grocery list, we have, albeit inadvertently, decreased our weight load by not fully engaging. When we perform rote actions as a teacher without our heart and mind in it, we need to hit the pause button. We might ask God how we can stretch and inspire our young charges. We need to pray to God to help us increase our weight load and alter our rote course to maximize our effectiveness for Him, just as Jesus Christ did for us. He didn't hand off His cross to someone else because He didn't feel like bearing the weight of the world's sin. He wasn't afraid to minister to women marginalized by society. He toppled the moneychangers' tables where cheating and stealing were occurring and turned protocol on its ear. He exhibited courage as He rejected the ease of accommodation. In fact, the antonym commonly listed for accommodation is *burden*. Jesus took on the burden of the world.

Are we willing to reject accommodations in the form of daily temptations and traps dispensed by the Enemy to take on the burdens He puts before us? If we say yes and pray for His help to accomplish it, we move closer to effective service. And we are assured He will share our burden and give us rest (Matthew 11:28).

Keys to Kingdom Living: Reject accommodation in order to be all you can be for God and His people.

Doorpost: "You yourselves, as living stones, are being built into a spiritual house for a holy priesthood to offer spiritual sacrifices acceptable to God through Jesus Christ." 1 Peter 2:5

THE INVESTMENT OF SPIRITUAL TRAINING: THE PRINCIPLE OF REVERSIBILITY

*L*et's be honest: when it comes to any proactive activity, there are going to be periods of dryness. The same is true in our walk with God. There are going to be days when, at the very least, we may not be in the mood to open our Bible and, at the very worst, may be in the depths of despair, questioning His very existence and wisdom regarding a disappointment. But just because we have landed there doesn't mean we are banished forever from contentment.

Whatever temptation or circumstance is trying to keep you from God, it's important to rail against the principle of *reversibility*. In personal training, this principle refers to the loss of beneficial effects of training when workouts cease. In short, "If you don't use it, you lose it." If we cease to exercise our fleshly bodies, areas once toned will atrophy and become flabby and nonresponsive.

Atrophy occurs in our spiritual life too. If we occasionally skip the mealtime prayer, it may easily become lost in the shuffle of family planning and rapid-fire banter. Before long, the act of giving thanks before breaking bread modeled by Jesus Himself is relegated to Christmas and Easter. Eventually, the mindfulness of the Supplier of our daily bread begins to evaporate. Without a reversal, the trend will continue in a downward spiral. Skipping worship, forgetting morning and evening prayers, and tithing may disappear, as well. The phrase "we don't drift toward holiness" is irrefutably true.

Thankfully, there are countless stories in the Bible of people whose lives were forever changed by positive reversals. The parable of the prodigal son in Luke 15 outlines how a young heir growing up in a godly home demanded his inheritance early, went his own way, and sank into a pit of despair so low he was forced to feed pigs and eat their leftover slop. Exercising the principle of reversibility, the son shed his attitude of pride for humility and went to his father to beg forgiveness, where he found it in unimaginable measure.

Jesus Christ's measure of forgiveness is also nearly incomprehensible. His entire ministry centered on the implementation of the principle of reversibility. He anticipated the principle of accommodation would play a role in every man and woman's life. He remains ready to invite those who don't follow Him to admit they are lost, repent of their wrongdoing, and accept the free grace available to all as a result of His death on the cross as a "ransom for many" (Mark 10:45). His death is the eraser that eradicates our mistakes, resulting in a clean sheet of paper available to us over and over again, no matter how many times we stumble and fall. The million-dollar question is, are we ready to engage the principle of reversibility? Vow today to let Jesus take the wheel, and trust Him to help you reverse your setbacks.

Keys to Kingdom Living: We can reverse our course when we let go and let Jesus.

Doorpost: "Throw off your old sinful nature and your former way of life. . . . Let the Spirit renew your thoughts and attitudes." Ephesians 4:22–23 (NLT)

THE INVESTMENT OF SPIRITUAL
TRAINING: THE PRINCIPLE OF REST

*T*he principle of *rest* stipulates that to make fitness gains, you must take time to recover. The idea is to avoid injury by overtraining. But it's also implied that the mind needs a break, too, to rejuvenate and get on board so it can work to maximum potential after a short respite.

On paper, observing the Sabbath and keeping it holy might seem like an easy commandment to keep, at least on the surface. But if we trot off to sporting events, cook and clean in advance for the rest of the week, or answer office emails all afternoon, are we really keeping that day holy? From the observance of the simple nap to the worship time with the Lord, all aspects of the Sabbath are equally important and part of the commandment laid out in Exodus 20:8–11.

Next time you feel burned out on life, familial duty, or ministry, take a look at your Sabbath "history." If you, any of your family members, livestock or any "foreigner who is within your gates" (v. 10) is working, the Sabbath is being violated. As for the many aspects of the Sabbath outlined in the book of Numbers, many Christians believe those aspects of the law were eradicated when the temple's curtain was torn in two (Matthew 27:50–51). Thankfully, we are under the Lord's umbrella of grace when it comes to keeping any commandment; we are sinners and fall short. And if you don't have control over your Sundays, set a goal to carve out a restful time devoted to the Lord on another day in your week. Spend it worshipping and focusing on Him. By doing so, you will be honoring the Sabbath in your own life. As 1 Samuel 16:7 reminds us, man looks at the outward appearance, but the Lord looks at the heart. God knows your intention to honor the Sabbath and cares more about that than He does about any calendar.

Of course, Christians and Jews disagree on the particulars of Sabbath observance. Ever since God instituted the Sabbath— requiring a day of rest for us, just as He rested after His six days of creating the world—men have been trying to get around it. In the Jewish faith, strict edicts stemming from the instructions in the book of Numbers are still a part of the faith walk, even if men continue to finagle their way around them. One such sidestep is the "Shabbat phone." Standard landlines and cell phones are designed with an electrical circuit which must be closed, or completed, for electricity to flow and a call to be connected. In some rabbinic teaching, completing a circuit falls under the same spirit as building something and, thus, is work[1] that's forbidden, so calls or texts made on those phones violate the Sabbath laws. As a result, a phone has been invented which is designed to barge in on an existing circuit so as not to complete anything on its own and, to the mind of the inventor, circumventing "completion." In the minds of some, this opens the door to conversation without violating the law. If that sounds ludicrous, there are thirty-eight other edicts that are referred to as the "39 Melachot" in traditional Jewish law.

How smug Shabbat phone inventors must feel. But God will not be mocked (Galatians 6:7). It's the heart attitude God looks for as we observe the Sabbath. Is our mind turned toward holiness? Do we keep God's commandment with joy? Or are we circumventing its purpose and trying to find ways around the letter of the law in violation of its spirit? Pray for God to lead you into daily moments of rest as well as ways to genuinely honor God on the Sabbath and recalibrate your energy level. And ask Him for discernment in all matters of obedience as you undertake the effort.

Keys to Kingdom Living: His divine design for a balanced life requires work and rest.

Doorpost: "By the seventh day God completed His work that He had done, and He rested on the seventh day from all His work that He had done. God blessed the seventh day and declared it holy, for on it He rested from His work of creation." Genesis 2:2–3

WEEK 4: SEVEN KEY VERSES

SEVEN KEY VERSES: JOHN 3:16

*J*t may seem trite to cite this familiar verse as one of the most important in the Bible, but the fact remains that it's the power bar of all Bible verses. When it's truly believed, it packs all the vital life-giving nutrients to truly nourish Christians and redeem nonbelievers from the pit. "For God so loved the world that He gave His only Son that whoever believes in Him will not perish, but have everlasting life."

This verse, often called "the gospel in a nutshell," is widely considered as an all-encompassing summary of the foundations of Christianity. In this precious sentence, we learn of God's ultimate sacrifice for us. His love for the sinners of the world was so great that He permitted His only perfect, blameless Son to be born, only to die on a cross to pay the price for our sin and shame. We are told that by putting our faith and trust in the redemptive story of Jesus Christ, we're spared from eternal death. Through that all-encompassing belief alone, and devoid of merit or deservedness, we're launched into God's plan for a joyous eternal life with Him.

I make it a point not to let the familiarity of this verse detract from the tremendous life-giving power it contains. No matter how many times we've seen it on a cardboard sign during a televised sports event, recited it at Sunday school, or read it in our Bible, its powerful truths can never be underestimated or undervalued. Ask any new Christian who unpacks it, and discover the beauty contained within it and the power of what it's done for them.

Nicodemus was the first seeker of truth to hear these powerful words. He had heard of the teachings of Jesus and met with Him at night so as not to be seen by the Jewish leaders of the day. He was a Pharisee and a member of the powerful Sanhedrin. We aren't ever clearly told that Nicodemus put his trust in Jesus. We do know that he stood up for justice in the law for people to be heard before being judged as temple leaders began making snap judgments about Jesus. Finally, we see Nicodemus's gift of embalming spices and his assistance in preparing Jesus's body for burial.

I look at Nicodemus and see a man whose actions spoke louder than his words. When many Christ-followers deserted Him in droves, Nicodemus publicly and boldly stood by Jesus during what seemed like the bitter end inside the tomb. How many followers praised Jesus on that Palm Sunday ride into Jerusalem, only to shout out cries of crucifixion days later?

These ancient words still bring amazing power to so many people even today. In a world where overachievement and performance are intrinsic to self-worth, Jesus offers hope for those who simply confess imperfections, put their trust in Him, and take the righteous leap of faith because of the joy, hope, and promises they exemplify. How marvelous it is that in God's economy, salvation is available to all.

Keys to Kingdom Living: Feel His love, believe in life everlasting, and prepare for that eternal life.

Doorpost: "But to all who did receive Him, He gave them the right to be children of God, to those who believe in His name." John 1:12

SEVEN KEY VERSES: JOHN 13:34

*s a young mother, I heard stories from other young moms about the funny things their kids would do. I remember one particularly amusing tale about a toddler who was a work-in-progress when it came to sharing. His mother would tell me of instances where she would ask for a bite of a cookie, and he would snag a pea-size morsel and proudly hand it to her. Or she would ask him for a french fry and he would dig down into the carton to pull out the smallest one he could find to place in her hand. Fortunately, he's grown leaps and bounds since those tiny-fry days and today is a considerate Christian young man.

True selfless sharing requires a lifelong commitment to surrendering ourselves. In John 13 Jesus speaks to His disciples. Prior to that moment, He had washed their feet, instituted the Last Supper, and explained its deep significance. As the weight of His suffering begins to descend on His sacrificial shoulders, Jesus shares with them a commandment reflecting the truth He's spent His whole life modeling: "I give you a new command: Love one another. Just as I have loved you, you must also love one another" (v. 34). He repeats the commandment again in John 15 and ups the stakes by adding, "No one has greater love than this, that someone would lay down his life for his friends" (John 15:13).

Loving with your last breath is undeniably a God-sized task. Christian theologian Oswald Chambers refers to this high level of love as "the loftiest preference of one person for another."[1] He goes on to say that "spiritually Jesus demands that this sovereign preference be for Himself."[2] Only when we love God with our whole heart can we even begin to try to love each other with the sacrificial love of handing over the "bigger fry."

Loving one another as Jesus loved us also involves loving others with acceptance of their imperfections. Jesus doesn't put conditions on His love for us or take exception with our faults and missteps. He loves us warts and all. And part of loving as He did is to love others with an all-in attitude. It wasn't until I became a mother that I realized how conditional my love, even for my children, could become if I didn't keep myself in check. I would be tempted to withdraw affection or approval when my firstborn didn't live up to my expectations or obey me unconditionally. And my youngest child, who is severely autistic, proved even more challenging to love in some ways because of his occasional propensity to become violent. Eventually it dawned on me that even though God is perfect, He never tries to expect perfection from His flawed people who could never deliver. That populous includes my imperfect self, just as it includes my family members.

Verses like the aforementioned John 13:34 remind us that when it comes to God-sized tasks, only God Himself can empower us with the desire and energy to attempt what is only possible under His guidance and in His immeasurable strength. May we experience an infusion of God-powered love so we can in turn love like Jesus does.

Keys to Kingdom Living: Strive to love others as Jesus sacrificially did—and still does.

Doorpost: "This is what I command you: Love one another." John 15:17

SEVEN KEY VERSES: LUKE 1:37

When the Virgin Mary learns she's been chosen to give birth to the long-awaited Messiah, she doesn't stand to take a bow or offer a lofty acceptance speech. She isn't grandstanding for a fan base for herself. Instead, she declares to an angel, in Luke 1:37, that "nothing will be impossible with God," and rightly shifts the glory onto Him. When Mary is told of the plan God has for her life, she valiantly embraces what seems impossible by reinforcing the truth of the plan. She praises God and His absolute power. She declares without reserve that He is more than capable of bringing it about, however preposterous the plan may appear on the surface.

Do we profess the same kind of blind faith when God puts a promise in front of us? God accomplishes the impossible in many ways. He executes His own plans that are usually much bigger than ours. He can plant a dream or idea in our minds and, when we follow His leadings, we can partner with Him to make it come to fruition.

God has done this many times in my life and in the lives of my spouse and children. When my husband had to choose from five job offers, we prayed together and the Lord led him to the job he was meant to have. As the years passed, we watched all the other firms who had extended offers suffered serious blows of one kind or another. God really did know what was best, and His dream for my husband's career proved to be the biggest.

He is also the God of the impossible when He plucks someone out of the depths of despair or evildoing. When He transforms them not only into children of God but effective evangelists, His divine providence shines brightly. He accomplished this with Paul back in the early days of Christianity and continues to do so today with individuals such as Lee Strobel, an atheist-turned-theologian and powerful kingdom worker.

Sometimes, however, our understanding of what God *can* do and what He *will* do gets muddled. This passage from Luke 1:37 is occasionally misinterpreted as a promise. Sometimes people read this and think to themselves that any idea or plan that occurs to them is going to be possible with God's help. God's power is unmatched—*that* we can be assured of. But sometimes, in the hatching of man-made plans, we haven't truly determined when, or if, God is on board (or, if we're on board with Him!). A seemingly impossible scheme hatched in our own mind might not be in alignment with what God wants for our lives. Our self-talk may lead us to believe that we are simply leaving something up to God to bring it about, even though our notion may never have been part of His plan at all. Staying in deep communion with God through prayer, reflection, and study of His word helps us to stay in alignment with all He wants to bring about in our lives when we keep our eyes on Him.

Keys to Kingdom Living: Recognize the God of the impossible when He brings leadings or dreams into your realm of possibilities, and pray to Him for them to come to fruition.

Doorpost: "What is impossible with men is possible with God." Luke 18:27

SEVEN KEY VERSES: MARK 16:15

*M*any people use technology to talk to others, even in their own home. I admit to one time where I texted my oldest when he still lived at home and was just upstairs. The first time I saw another mother do this, I thought how ridiculous it was. Before I knew it, I was doing just that.

The words of Jesus recorded in Mark were received with great zeal at the time. Procrastination didn't rear its ugly head. These guys literally hit the road. It strikes me as ironic. Jesus told the disciples, "Go into all the world and preach the gospel to the whole creation" (Mark 16:15). They were to bring the good news to those who hadn't heard it yet. At a time when conversation and letters were the only forms of communication, this was a huge request. It proved to be a vast undertaking for the eleven men standing before Jesus. It's not like they had a fleet of chariots or a bevy of camels or donkeys at their disposal. They had one mode of transportation: their feet. Yet they traversed the ancient world, including Europe and the Near and Middle East, without a second thought, sacrificing comfort, security, and even family concerns.

Today we can fly across the globe and back in less than a week. Yet many modern-day roadblocks to the idea of going and telling the good news still prove problematic. All roadblocks to witnessing have one obstacle in common: the self. Giving up a week on the beach for a week serving in Africa involves dismantling a roadblock of the self. A sacrifice of self and pride may be involved when we try to bring the good news to someone who continually rejects our delivery. We may find ourselves torn between buying a new sports car or funding an overseas mission trip.

We need to be in constant prayer about where God is leading us to deliver His good news. Whether we are led to go down the street or across town, to traverse the state or country, or to hop on a plane to fly across the globe, we should continually be looking for opportunities. And if we are limited in our mobility, we can still dedicate funds for others, donate supplies, knit blankets, and pray for those who are being led to undertake the actual travel. The beauty of God's hands and feet working together to accomplish the final task given by Jesus Himself is that they all work in tandem to bring about the ultimate result: reaching one more for Jesus.

Where is God leading you to donate your time, talents, and treasure? Will you bury your head in the sand like an ostrich? Or will you launch yourself out of your comfortable nest "on wings like eagles," as we read in Isaiah 40:31? Those who do will "run and not grow weary; they will walk and not faint."

Keys to Kingdom Living: Take the words of Jesus's Great Commission seriously, implementing your heart, soul, and mind to bring joy and hope to our lost world.

Doorpost: "Go into all the world and preach the gospel to the whole creation." Mark 16:15

SEVEN KEY VERSES:
EPHESIANS 3:18–19

*M*ost of man's greatest inhumanities to man can be attributed, to some degree, to a lack of fully internalizing God's love. Even some Christians fail to fathom the tremendous largesse of the Creator's love for all His creation. When we fail to love and honor what God loves, we miss out on all God wants for us in our lives. We all need God's perfect love, a love that is freely given to all He created.

These Ephesians verses are the first Bible passage I ever chose to pray on its own without adding any of my own words. The words leaped from the page one day as I was studying God's Word. Paul prayed that the people of Ephesus would "comprehend with all the saints what is the length and width, height and depth of God's love, and to know the Messiah's love that surpasses knowledge, so [they] may be filled with all the fullness of God."

The timing of this exercise was perfect. It was a difficult year in my life. I faced the loss of a friendship that meant more to me than it did to the other person, disappointments with my children, and challenges with my family of origin. These blows caused me to further isolate myself. When I had sunk into a pit so deep I couldn't climb out by myself, or whenever I felt despondency coming on, I began to pray those words daily, and sometimes more than once a day.

There was no "aha" moment or watershed experience that left me instantaneously changed. But what I did experience over the course of ten months was a slow yet deeply rooted paradigm shift. Although I had known since I was a child that "Jesus loves me," the internalizing of that love was far more limited in my heart than in my mind.

I noticed the change in small ways at first, like when someone in my life would disappoint me. Instead of becoming derailed by it, I would be reminded how God's love is my all-in-all—all that I really need. Love from others, even family members, became more "gravy" than "main dish." I enjoyed it but didn't need or demand it in the same way. And activities, like sitting by myself in church, used to make me sad. Now when I sit by myself in a sanctuary, I feel God fully and completely, whether I'm on an emotional mountaintop or in a deep valley. I can feel His love run through my veins and swell in my heart until it feels as if it might burst. But the biggest change in my life since this promise has come to fruition for me is how I'm no longer easily derailed by circumstances. God's love is my sustenance and the "superglue" that holds me together. Deep cracks that threatened to crumble me before are now just barely visible surface fissures. I can feel how wide and how deep God's love is for me. That it is the only love that truly conquers any circumstance or disappointment.

Keys to Kingdom Living: Pray this Scripture and thank God in advance for what He'll do next!

Doorpost: "Everyone who loves has been born of God and knows God. The one who does not love does not know God, because God is love." 1 John 4:7–8

SEVEN KEY VERSES: ISAIAH 41:10

I delude myself into believing I am fearless. Sometimes when I think about "fearing not," I dismiss the caution as non-applicable to my life. In such ludicrous moments of self-deceptive arrogance, I am able to fool myself. I reduce the meaning of fear to a reactive full-blown personal terror or a heightened state of individual alert. But the truth is that whenever I start to worry, to lash out at someone, or to avoid problems or duties, I'm experiencing fear of some kind.

While it isn't a sin to fear, the perpetuation of a fearful existence is evidence of a lack of trust in God. I love the translation of this powerful verse from Isaiah about fear in The Message Bible. It reads, "Don't panic. I'm with you. There's no need to fear for I'm your God. I'll give you strength. I'll help you. I'll hold you steady, keep a firm grip on you" (Isaiah 41:10).

Panic is a kind of "zero to sixty" emotion that can rapidly escalate if we don't keep it in check. A friend once shared with me that she always tries to picture Jesus seated next to her. She might imagine Him in the passenger seat of her car while driving to an important meeting or medical appointment that is causing her anxiety. If we visually remind ourselves of what our head knowledge already accepts, it helps us feel His presence in a more powerful way.

When we look at the words "I'm your God," we are reminded of His sovereignty. The verse promises He will give us strength;

clearly, there is no better source for that than God Himself. We also read that He will help us. When I think of God helping me, I'm reminded of that beautiful verse in Psalm 121: "I look up to the mountains; does my strength come from mountains? No, my strength comes from God, who made heaven, and earth, and mountains" (v. 1–2). If God can make the heaven and earth, He is fully capable of moving mountains for you.

Most importantly, God promises that He will hold us steady. When we trust God and rest ourselves in the palm of His hand, we won't lose our balance and fall or topple over. The verse also says He will keep a firm grip on us.

How firm is God's grip? We're told in John 10:28 that no one will snatch us out of the Father's hand. What a comfort this verse is when we see friends or loved ones who've wandered away from God and His promises; we're told here that anyone who once truly belonged to God cannot be fully removed. We can take that promise to the vault and on into eternity.

While it's true we won't ever be able to fully remove fear from our lives this side of eternity, we can choose to respond to fearful moments and situations by trusting God to bring us through them. We can ask Him through prayer and petition to allow His perfect peace to live and reign in our lives. When do this, we enjoy the deep bond our Father God intended for us. Then we can model this supernatural courage for those still lost in darkness.

Keys to Kingdom Living: Cast out fear by trusting in God.

Doorpost: "Do not fear, for I am with you." Isaiah 41:10

SEVEN KEY VERSES: MATTHEW 28:20

*I*n our troubled world, it's easy to wake up in the morning and feel defeated enough to pull the covers over our heads. It's far more challenging to rejoice about the day that's about to unfold, even if we are told in Psalm 118:24 that "this is the day the Lord has made; let us rejoice and be glad in it." We are to be glad *in* the day, even if we aren't so thrilled about it, simply because God Himself has made it.

God knew from the dawn of time this would prove to be a daunting task. He took significant steps to help us counteract our pessimism with Bible verses about the importance of how to best tackle our days from the get-go. God knew we would be tempted to open our newspapers before our Bibles, that we would squabble with family members in the early hours of the day, or that the tragedy we dealt with the day before would be fresh on our minds once the sunrise loomed on the horizon.

That's why Jesus's parting words before He ascended into heaven after rising from the dead were so carefully chosen by Him. He wanted to counteract the defeatist feelings that so often descend on us like a black thundercloud. In today's key Scripture, Matthew 28:20, Jesus leaves His followers, uttering these powerful words: "And remember, I am with you always, to the end of the age." In a world where seeing was—and still is—believing, Jesus rises into the clouds, all the while proclaiming He is with us always.

The other important thing God did to drive home the point that He is always with us is to remind us that we can commune with Him whenever we want. When Jesus died on the cross, the debt we could never pay was settled and our redemption won. We are told in Hebrews 4:16 that because of this sacrificial love, we can boldly approach the throne with confidence.

Jesus Himself modeled this for the disciples when He would withdraw to be alone with the Father. We, too, need to withdraw and be alone with Him every day, preferably in the morning, before headlines, deadlines, and the fault lines of our relationships threaten to crack our composure. We need to transform ourselves with the renewing of our mind daily (Romans 12:2), reminding ourselves that God is in control. We would do well to focus on God's sovereignty at the crack of dawn before we begin to feel ourselves unraveling over the sad state of domestic and world affairs. When it seems like we can't take one more day inside our home sanctuary that sometimes feels more like a battlefield at times, we can recall that He is Immanuel: God with us. When hurricanes, earthquakes, floods, droughts, pandemics, and tsunamis threaten our planet and seem to bring Armageddon ever closer, we can rest assured, knowing Jesus Christ promised His powerful presence can be counted on until the last breath on earth is drawn. Will you commit to remaining mindful of God's powerful presence daily?

Keys to Kingdom Living: God vows to be with us always!

Doorpost: "I will never leave you or forsake you." Hebrews 13:5

WEEK 5: INVESTING IN SECURITY

INVESTING IN SECURITY: GUARD!

$\mathcal{W}$ho doesn't remember Linus, the Peanuts character? He was always dragging around his "trusty blanket," as he called it. Linus dragged around this textile panacea wherever he went, confidently justifying its presence to anyone who tried to criticize him for continually toting it around.

Security blankets can take on a number of forms. Some are as obvious as fat bank accounts or legal documents. Others might be more subtle in nature, like fawning entourages, an athlete's pre-batting ritual, or a good luck charm. A case could be made that drugs, alcohol, and even sex may serve as a security blanket. Such objects, substances, and activities are often abused by adults to alleviate their stress and anxiety. Indeed, it's human nature to gravitate to what may make us feel secure.

But in truth, the only genuine security available to us is a hope and a future in Jesus Christ. He is the only Security Guard in whom we can place our total trust. In John 10:11, Jesus tells of the Good Shepherd who lays down His life for the sheep. He secured an eternal destiny for all mankind when He shed His blood on the cross to atone for our sins. When we acknowledge this, repent, and receive His grace, we enjoy the 24/7 security that nothing can snatch us out of His protective hand (John 10:28).

Our heavenly Security Guard not only watches over us, He has a security detail in place that we can't even see. He tells you in Psalm 91:11 that He has placed angels in charge of you so that you will "not dash your foot against a stone" (v. 12) There are many stories in the Bible of angels ministering to saints. In Matthew 18 we read how they guard children. And an angel ministered to Jesus after he was tempted, in Matthew 4:11.

Eternal security doesn't guarantee that nothing bad will ever happen to us on earth. But God does guarantee our eternal security and promises in Psalm 91 verses 15 and 16, that "I will be with him in trouble. I will rescue him and give him honor . . . and show him My salvation." The security of knowing we cannot be irreparably harmed is a great comfort, when we fully internalize it. We can trust that no matter what hardship we endure, our divine destiny is forever sealed.

Some atheists believe Christians use God as a security blanket. They argue that a divine being serves as an imagined safety net. They claim Christians can't face a world without a divine being and therefore trust in something they cannot see as a defense mechanism. They are only partly right in that assessment. To a Christian, life in this broken world is unimaginable without God. But God isn't our defense mechanism; He *is* our defense, and our "ever present help in trouble," as we read in Psalm 46:1.

Keys to Kingdom Living: Toss aside false securities and cling to Jehovah Jireh, our provider.

Doorpost: "May the God of hope fill you with all joy and peace as you believe in Him, so that you may overflow with hope by the power of the Holy Spirit." Romans 15:13

INVESTING IN SECURITY: IN OUR
FINAL DESTINATION

*J*t's a bittersweet rite of passage when a child that once delighted in the magic of toys suddenly prefers gift cards for gasoline and peppermint lattes. There's not much of a Kodak moment involved in envelope ripping. Thank heavens for grandchildren and the ability to start the toy process anew with the next generation.

While I admit the idea of shopping with a gift card is exciting, I must confess I have a hard time trusting its process. When I am buying them for others, I'm always a little anxious that they aren't being loaded properly or that there are going to be hidden restrictions. And as a recipient, I have occasionally tried to use one at a store where there's a glitch on the register refusing it one minute and inexplicably taking it moments later.

Thankfully, our most important divine transaction is bathed in a security level that cannot be compromised by anyone or anything. When we give our hearts to Jesus, God seals the deal for our eternal destiny. We are told in Romans 11:29 that the gifts of God are irrevocable. The gifts of redemption from the pit, absolution, peace that passes all understanding, community with other believers, being grafted into His forever family, the restoration of our earthly bodies, and our immortal destiny are gifts that really do keep on giving and never lose their priceless value.

From time to time, committed Christians may struggle with that assurance. My mother wrestled with such nagging feelings of doubt. As she deteriorated from lung cancer that had spread to her brain, she would say things like, "Well, I hope I'm going to heaven." When I would reassure her that she didn't need to have any doubts, she would sort of nod her head without seeming fully convinced, as if she worried about some fine print keeping her out of the pearly gates.

One obstruction to assurance involves misguided notions that performance plays a part in our salvation. Some Christians mistakenly believe their checklist of earthly service lacks the requisite good deeds or that they aren't devout enough or obedient enough. Though consciously we know salvation is a free gift from God (Romans 6:23), the temptation to de-emphasize grace can actually strangle our hope—and perhaps, in some cases, our salvation—if it isn't rooted in redemption and repentance.

We need to be truly mindful of the blessed assurance that not only is Jesus ours, but we are His! One of the most comforting passages in the Bible, Romans 8:38–39, reminds us of the important truth that "not even death or life, angels or rulers, things present or things to come . . . or any other created thing will have the power to separate us from the love of God that is in Christ Jesus our Lord!" And that's the most important treasure we can store in our vaults.

Keys to Kingdom Living: The eternal security of authentic believers is fully assured.

Doorpost: "Everyone the Father gives Me will come to Me, and the one who comes to Me I will never cast out." John 6:37

INVESTING IN SECURITY: IN THE TOTALITY OF OUR REDEMPTION

From the time we are small children, we learn to understand the cycle of wrongdoing. If we are raised in a moral household, we are led by example to experience remorse. This is hopefully followed by admission of guilt and perhaps a form of atonement followed by forgiveness and, in some cases, restitution. Of course, many people who lack moral character might provide the lip service of saying they are sorry without truly meaning it or, worse yet, not even admitting or apologizing for any wrongdoing.

In today's culture, some wrongdoing is even boasted about and heralded as a coup on the part of the perpetrator. Take eighty-five-year-old jewel thief Doris Payne. She boasted for decades about her five-finger capers in luxury department and jewelry stores. In a 2016 interview with the Associated Press, she expressed delight about a brewing development deal for a film about her life. "I know what I've done. I'm not too ashamed of it," she was quoted as saying.[1]

Genuine Christians understand the benefits of repentance and forgiveness. They strive for obedience. They try to lead a life that is pleasing to God. Of course, we all "sin and fall short" of that goal, as we read in Romans 3:23. We are told repeatedly in Scripture that our sins are forgiven when we go before our Lord with a contrite heart, confess our wrongdoing, and receive the grace and absolution only He can give. We can feel remorse and shame for what we have done, but we don't need to freeze like petrified wood. When we sit in our shame long after it has reached its expiration date, we are falling victim to Satan's scheme to render us ineffective. Anyone who has been born already has Christ's sacrifice available, their sins forgiven and their debt paid by Christ on the cross. The step we take to obtain this gift is found in Acts 3:19, where we're directed to repent and turn to God so our sins will be wiped out. In 1 Corinthians 6:11 we are told we were washed, sanctified, and justified "in the name of the Lord Jesus Christ and by the Spirit of our God." When Jesus Christ replaced condemnation with grace more than two thousand years ago, He won your battle before you had even been born!

It's important to resist the festering, lingering feelings of shame. They aren't part of God's plan for your life. He wants you to move forward on both feet, not to keep one stuck in the past. The praise band Big Daddy Weave's "Redeemed" song speaks of this very condition, with lyrics describing being "bound up in shackles" of our failures. God doesn't want our list of transgressions to stalk us. We don't need to be a prisoner of war; we can "stop fighting a fight that's already been won," as the praise song states. The "voice of shame and regret" they speak of is replaced by the encouraging words in 2 Corinthians 5:17 that remind us that "if anyone is in Christ, he is a new creation; old things have passed away, and look, new things have come."

Keys to Kingdom Living: Remain confident knowing you're permanently redeemed when you repent and accept the free grace of God through forgiveness.

Doorpost: "There is no fear in love; instead, perfect love drives out fear, because fear involves punishment. So the one who fears has not reached perfection in love." 1 John 4:18

INVESTING IN SECURITY: IN BEING LOVED

Our primal need for love is deep seated. We are born into this world with a God-shaped hole that only He can successfully fill. It is an integral part of God's plan to mold us for relationship with Him and then with one another. His divine plan centers around a home featuring a loving mother and father who are committed to each other for life as well as to the one true God. Together, mother and father provide love and security while setting healthy boundaries as they prepare their offspring for successful launches into the world. Ideally, the children themselves can one day be effective parents and kingdom workers like their parents before them.

Of course, we all know this scenario could not be farther from the norm, as so many families today reflect our broken world. And the trouble doesn't just stop there. Popular culture and the media in particular are keen on steering our desires to many other substitutes vying to fill our God-shaped holes. Satan loves to dangle inferior substitutes, such as fame, fortune, and power in front of the chronically dissatisfied. More subtle substitutes are those deemed socially acceptable such as idealized romantic or parental love. Problems arise when anything else occupies the top spot God requires in our lives. Young girls fed a steady diet of shows like *The Bachelor* crave a highly idyllic, manufactured form of romantic love. That's nearly impossible to achieve outside of carefully crafted reality television. And the parents who pour their entire hearts and souls, as well as their Sundays, into their children's social lives, sports schedules, and academic pursuits also set themselves up for potential estrangement from each other and eventually from God.

The good news is that unlike all other forms of love, God's love truly is perfect. It is never conditional, never vacillates, and is never dependent on circumstances or reciprocity. God loves those who don't love Him just as much as He loves those who do. When we internalize the full extent of God's love, we can feel the wind beneath our wings to such a life-changing degree that it transcends all our expectations. In no other area of life can such expectations be fulfilled.

A couple of years back, I struggled with feelings of acceptance and love from those around me. During a Bible study of Ephesians, I began to pray that God would help me to deeply feel His love to such an extent that I would be able to literally live on it. I made up my mind that the love I received from friends and family members would be the gravy, and that God would be the main dish, my all-in-all, my pot roast.

This didn't happen overnight. I began to pray Ephesians 3:18 over and over again. Over a period of months, I experienced a transformation in my life. My thoughts about sitting occasionally by myself in church began to shift. I felt an intensified level of intimacy and communion between God and myself. Through prayer and petition, and increased time in the Word and in His presence, my feelings matched God's promises. Yes, Jesus loves me! After years of simply singing these words, I finally understood and internalized them.

Keys to Kingdom Living: Capitalize on the full measure of God's perfect love.

Doorpost: "I pray that you, being rooted and firmly established in love, may be able to comprehend with all the saints what is the length and width, height and depth of God's love." Ephesians 3:17–18

INVESTING IN SECURITY: IN
FOLLOWING THE LAW

*I*t is widely accepted in the field of psychology that fear of the unknown ranks in the top three deep-seated human fears, directly behind death and public speaking.

Children in particular tend to thrive best when they understand exactly what is expected of them—and what is not. When a child learns rules in his family of origin, he's able to think in an orderly way about what is permissible and what isn't in any given moment, fostering a spirit of cooperation between himself and his parents. And because most rules are in place to protect the child and his fellow human beings, rules also keep him and others safe. Finally, as a keeper of the rules, the child submits to authority during his period of growth and transition until he moves out on his own and the followed rules become a part of who he is as a citizen of the world. For the child and the parent, the act of submission is more important than the track record of keeping the rules.

As children of God, we too are nestled within a secure framework of God's laws. God's commandments provide a structure for us to conform to, and even though we are not, in our flawed humanity, able to perfectly follow them, we do our best out of love for our Father. Like our own children, we are also more secure when we know what is expected of us. Paul understood this well when he spoke of freedom in the law. Though these two terms seem contradictory, Paul speaks at great length about what it really means to be free in Christ, striving for obedience—but, more importantly, achieving restoration through grace. In Romans 8:21 Paul writes about how we are set free from the bondage and corruption of our sin, from before we were repentant, and redeemed to where we obtain "the glorious freedom of God's children."

Our success in following Jesus Christ, then, is no longer dependent on our ability to keep the law but in our freedom from condemnation under it. This came to mind the other day as I sat for a long time in my office chair. I often tuck one of my legs under me while I work. Eventually, the leg that is pressed upon becomes numb and feels cut off from the rest of my body. When it is numb, it cannot freely move. But when I free it from the weight of the rest of me, it begins to revive, regaining blood flow and becoming useful again. If we don't repent or accept God's grace, our sinful "leg" remains dead and useless. But when we embrace the salvation plan of Jesus Christ, our limb is free from the weight of condemnation and is able to thrive as God intended.

Like the limb set free, we have the ability to move and to please God when we put off the weight of our sin nature. We can be released from bondage to pursue righteousness.

Keys to Kingdom Living: In Christ we are free from condemnation, secure in His redemptive plan, and nestled in relationship with Him as we set our intention to please and obey Him.

Doorpost: "But the one who looks intently into the perfect law of freedom and perseveres in it, and is not a forgetful hearer but one who does good works—this person will be blessed in what he does." James 1:25

INVESTING IN SECURITY: IN FOLLOWING HIS WILL

*R*emember the Magic 8 Ball toy that gave answers to questions when it was tipped down and then up again? Throughout history, the ill-conceived desire to know the future has been played out with tea leaves, horoscopes, tarot cards, fortune cookies, and a seemingly endless array of methods. People vacillate with choices and decisions and sometimes look for guidance in all the wrong places.

Christians can remain confident in the knowledge that their only beacon of light in the darkness of the unknown lies in Jesus Christ. He is the light of the world, as He tells us in John 8:12. When we look to Him for guidance and direction, we can be assured of the security in knowing we are doing His will in our lives, step by step.

I don't know about you, but I'm relieved I was never handed a blueprint of my life once I was able to read. I would have been ill-prepared for the information about the tragedies that would occur in my life, and even about some of the successes. Despair would no doubt have ensued with the bad news, and pride may have insinuated itself with the good. We are ill-equipped to deal with such revelations. And this is one of the reasons we are told in Matthew 6:34 not to worry about tomorrow, for "each day has enough trouble of its own." In the verse that precedes this one, Jesus tells us to seek His kingdom and His righteousness first before concerning ourselves with anything else.

When Daniel experienced visions of the future, he was far from elated at what he learned. He speaks of his experience in Daniel 10:8, saying "I was left alone, looking at this great vision. No strength was left in me; my face grew deathly pale, and I was powerless." He states in 10:2 that he mourned for three weeks after one of the visions was revealed to him.

We need to trust God's will for our lives. He knows far better than we do about what we can handle and what we can't when it comes to our present and our future. If we remain in prayer and communion with Him regarding all our decisions, big or small, we can trust Him completely to guide and direct us. Trying to go against His divine navigation would be like driving in the dark without headlights or a map. Only God has the map of our life from beginning to end. His is the only light we need rely on to illuminate our path, whether it's inch by inch or step by step through difficult situations. We don't need to focus on how much information we possess in a given situation, or even how spritely our gait may or may not need to be to line up with God's timing. We can fully depend on God to walk us through whatever we face. Whether we are sprinting along joyfully, dragging our feet, or being carried by Him completely, He will provide what we need to grow in our faith walk with Him.

Keys to Kingdom Living: Our future security rests not in gimmicks, games, or talismans, but in following God's will for our lives.

Doorpost: "I will instruct you and show you the way to go; with My eye on you, I will give counsel." Psalm 32:8

INVESTING IN SECURITY: IN OUR
IDENTITY IN CHRIST

remember the first time I traveled to New York as a reporter to cover New York Fashion Week. I'd received the beautiful invitations at my office months before and could hardly believe that my name had been printed on the envelopes mailed from some of America's most prestigious fashion houses.

Back in the '80s, if you weren't a wealthy socialite or celebrity, the seating hierarchy was based on the size and importance of your newspaper or magazine. Sometimes the designer held more than one show to accommodate everyone who needed to be included. Yet, even with multiple showings, some reporters from smaller towns were inevitably left out in the cold.

As a reporter from Houston, I did not make the A-list first show for Calvin Klein, though many of my more influential friends possessed the coveted ticket. I can still remember that feeling of not belonging as my colleagues shuffled out of the show and went off to write their stories. Trying to remain unruffled, I went to the second show that immediately followed the first. After it was over, I was filing out and the third-show invitees were nudging past me. I then noticed that the once-coveted invites completely littered the floor, amounting to little more than an elegant layer of refuse.

Unlike Calvin Klein, God structures entrance to His celestial surroundings around a framework of inclusion rather than exclusion. We are "a chosen race, a royal priesthood, a holy nation, a people for His own possession," as we learn in 1 Peter 2:9. Christ lives in us, as we learn in Galatians 2:20. We are God's chosen ones, from Colossians 3:12. He has put His seal on us, as we learn in 2 Corinthians 1:22. Our names are engraved in the Book of Life (Revelation 3:5). Our "invite" can never be rescinded once we genuinely and authentically commit ourselves to Jesus Christ with our whole heart.

As those who identify with Christ, we must make it our mission to share the good news of inclusiveness with those who have not yet RSVP'd to Him. We learn in Matthew 22 of a wedding banquet with a person who tried to crash the party. (Let's just say that it didn't go well for him!) We are assured of our identity in Christ once we commit to Him. Indeed, there won't be any wedding crashers in heaven. Our Good Shepherd knows His sheep. In Matthew 25:31–46, we learn He'll divide "invited" sheep from "wedding crasher" goats. While Jesus died for the sins of all mankind, both sheep and goats, each individual must decide whether or not to accept His invitation for salvation and eternal glory. Each will be accountable for accepting or denying an identity in Christ. No one will be able to ignore the invitation or slip in later. We must each RSVP for ourselves and tell others about the Host and all He offers to those identifying with Him. Make sure your invite and RSVP are secure in your vault.

Keys to Kingdom Living: We are included with, and identify with, Jesus when we invite Him into our hearts.

Doorpost: "All those led by God's Spirit are God's sons. . . . You received the Spirit of adoption." Romans 8:14–15

WEEK 6: VALUABLE LESSONS FROM CREATION

VALUABLE LESSONS FROM CREATION:
THE SERPENT

*E*ve's temptation to eat the forbidden fruit in Genesis 3 began innocently enough, at least to her untrained eye. A serpent hanging out in a tree asks her a probing question about God's only rule in the garden. This opens up what Satan hopes will be a diabolical dialogue on the possibilities of breaking that one rule. Eve won't really *die* if she eats the fruit of the tree, Satan maintains. These kinds of half-truths lie at the hallmark of Satan's deceptions. He wants nothing more than to minimize any potential wrongdoing you are considering in the hopes that you will stumble, too.

Once Eve and Adam have taken the infamous bites out of the piece of forbidden fruit, consequences are levied. After Eve blames the serpent for deceiving her, God says the snake is to be cursed more than any livestock and more than any wild animal (Genesis 3:14). When He says "on your belly you shall go," in the New King James version, God is implying that the serpent may have had limbs to travel in an upright manner prior to the garden encounter.

God goes on to describe the consequences to Satan himself, saying that his head will be bruised, but only Jesus's heel will be bruised, implying that both sides will incur a cost but Jesus will emerge the victor.

It might be tempting to think that the serpent is an innocent victim in Satan's plan if he entered into the unwitting animal.

However, we cannot begin to understand the mind of God. We do know that in Genesis 1:26 God says His plan for man was to "rule the fish of the sea, the birds of the sky, the livestock, all the earth, and the creatures that crawl on the earth." There is a certain irony that one of the creatures man supposedly had dominion over proved to be an integral part of his downfall.

We can learn much from the tragic garden scene. We see that the act of blaming is a time-honored early component in every man's flee from accountability. Adam blamed Eve, while Eve blamed the serpent. We also see from the way God dealt with the serpent that its actions have a cost. Anyone or anything involved in leading another down a path of wrongdoing pays a price, from the creature to Satan himself. When we are instrumental in causing anyone to stumble into sin, we are accountable, as well, for what happens to that person.

Even today, the snake remains greatly reviled. And as Christians, while we know Satan has a foothold in this world, we can rest assured that the "heel" that was bruised rose to heaven to be reunited with His Father.

The day is coming when Jesus Christ will return in all His glory. No doubt the serpent will be among all the "creatures on the earth and under the earth," referred to in Revelation 5:13, who will say "Blessing and honor and glory and dominion to the One seated on the throne, and to the Lamb, forever and ever!"

Keys to Kingdom Living: Remain on guard for temptation's origins and subtleties.

Doorpost: "Now the serpent was the most cunning of all the wild animals that the LORD God had made." Genesis 3:1

VALUABLE LESSONS FROM CREATION:
THE REMNANT, TWO BY TWO

*W*hen I stop to really think about the enormous undertaking of Noah, it boggles my mind. First, he had to build one of the biggest ships in history to house a remnant of mankind and flora and fauna according to God's specifications and standards. He had to build what must have looked like a spaceship in front of neighbors and friends who had never seen rain. They surely thought he was stark raving mad—until it started coming down in buckets. Then for forty days and forty nights, he and his family had to clean the stalls where the animals resided—and perhaps even propagated—during their little cruise. I wonder if Noah ever again had a hankering for sailing after that daunting little excursion. Thinking of the whole ordeal gives the term "poop deck" a whole new meaning.

These are, of course, my own musings. The account in Genesis reveals primarily the facts and specifics of God's plan to eradicate what He considered corrupt and still preserve a remnant. For the ark itself, He specified the material, the size of each of the three levels, and the purpose for each. Noah was to bring only his own family. As for the animals, he was to bring a male and a female into the ark to ensure the survival and propagation of the species.

Even in light of the cataclysmic chaos to come, God was in control. His plan was as ironclad as it was divinely inspired. From the dawn of creation, God created a male and a female from every species of animal. When it came to the creation of male and female, His order of things did not change. If Noah had brought two males or two females of the same species on board, that species would not be alive today. God's divine, superior order of pairing instituted on the day of creation was the same on the day Noah boarded the animals—and it remains the same today.

We can also learn from this account of Noah that man does have dominion over creation. He is entrusted with the responsibility of not just the day-to-day care of what God created but the preservation of the species for future generations. We must be good stewards of all God made to the best of our ability. However, we would do well to remember that Noah obeyed Genesis 1:26 by ruling over the animals as God instructed.

Thankfully, God promised never to send a flood again to destroy the face of the earth and all its inhabitants. Every time we see a rainbow, we can remind ourselves of how God preserved not just us but all the wildly diverse animals and plants which we can, and will, continue to enjoy, knowing God is a faithful promise keeper.

Keys to Kingdom Living: God's divine order is preserved even in His righteous indignation.

Doorpost: "You are also to bring into the ark two of all the living creatures, male and female, to keep them alive with you." Genesis 6:19

VALUABLE LESSONS FROM CREATION:
SACRIFICIAL ANIMALS

*T*he concept of sacrifice no longer carries with it a badge of honor, at least where the general public is concerned. Advertisements encourage indulgence, not self-denial. It's clear to any female over the age of fifteen that the model in the bikini doesn't regularly consume the greasy burger she holds in her manicured hand. So it's no surprise that when it comes to the topic of animal sacrifice in the Bible, controversy is expected to rear its ugly head. The idea of laying an innocent animal on a rock and sacrificing its life to its Creator may be a daunting one, but God had His reasons, and His Word clearly lays them out.

Animal lovers are still inclined to question the justification for these sacrifices, but a closer study of God's Word reveals many reasons they were required. A scanning of Leviticus 4 and 5 spells out in great detail the need for the shedding of blood to cover our sins and accompany God's merciful act of forgiveness. To be sure, God's ways are not our ways, but God's requirement for atonement prior to Jesus's death on the cross was the price He set for the mercy He was not required to provide but which He did out of a loving heart.

Perhaps the most important reason God instituted this practice is so that people of the time could experience what it meant to sacrifice something they truly cared about. I remember high school friends who were a part of the 4-H program. 4-H educates students who raise livestock and then arrange for the sale of the animal, either for breeding or for slaughter, to consumers who want to support the program and the students involved. The program helped train young people in animal care and served a need in the public for locally grown meat products. But for some students, letting go of their animals was harder than they imagined. My neighbor raised cows as a teenager, and to this day he cannot bring himself to eat veal because of the memory of caring for his young charges.

God's institution of the sacrificial animal involved the same kind of personal stakes. In Exodus 12:5–6, we read the edict from God calling for a year-old male animal without defect, either a sheep or a goat, to be cared for by the family, in their home, for a four-day period before it would then be slaughtered at twilight. This period of attachment served God's purpose of not just a property sacrifice; it was the one atoning who had a personal stake as well because of their love for the animal. God had an immense personal stake in the Sacrificial Lamb He offered for the atonement for our sins—His one and only Son!

When we put ourselves in God's shoes, we ponder what it must have been like to make the tremendous sacrifice of His own Son. We are put in our place as the grateful recipient of wholly underserved mercy and grace. These gifts from God came at a great price. We should thank Him daily on bended knee for all He's done for us.

Keys to Kingdom Living: Sacrificial animals paved the way for the Lamb of God.

Doorpost: "Here is the Lamb of God, who takes away the sin of the world!" John 1:29

VALUABLE LESSONS FROM CREATION:
JESUS'S BITTERSWEET DONKEY RIDE

*W*hen it comes to international jetsetters, travel budgets know no bounds. If the Sultan of Brunei is hit with a bout of wanderlust, he simply summons one of his six planes and two choppers to take him from point *A* to point *B*. Many Arab playboys have been known to fly their exotic sports cars with them in an Airbus A330. This enables them to drive it in the wee hours of the morning on the streets of London during their multi-week summer vacations.

But when the Son of God needed a ride into Jerusalem, He didn't glide in on a chariot, a noble steed, or even a camel. Instead, He rode in on a young donkey colt, fulfilling the prophecy of Zechariah 9:9. It states, "Your King is coming to you; He is righteous and victorious, humble and riding on a donkey." Of course, Jesus's approach was always subservient. He "made himself as nothing, by taking on the very nature of a servant, being made in human likeness" and "humbled himself by becoming obedient to death" as we read in Philippians 2:7–8.

Jesus's approach to the trappings of the world bore sharp contrast to the Pharisees of the time. While the Son of Man had "no place to lay His head," as recorded in Matthew 8:20, the priests of the day lived in mosaic-laden mansions with elaborately painted stucco walls replete with elaborate carvings. Each of their rooms was filled with the finest interior furnishings. Their luxurious carved-stone dining tables were adorned with fine tableware and glassware. All these trappings were paid for by the steep temple taxes levied on the citizens, many of whom struggled to make ends meet.

The choice of a donkey was more than just a nod to humility. We learn in 1 Kings 1:33 that it was an animal that communicated peace when Solomon rode one and was recognized as the king of Israel. Furthermore, donkeys are very intelligent, and although it's not widely known, they are actually stronger than a horse of the same size. Though to many, Jesus appeared vulnerable precisely because He did cloak Himself in humility in so many ways, He, too, was in fact far stronger than those to whom he was compared—though appearances at the time were deliberately deceiving.

Jesus, then and now, doesn't appear with an entourage courting the paparazzi, demanding notice or attention. He seeks those with hearts desiring to find Him. Those hearts are poised to embrace the peace and freedom He offers. Those who humble themselves in this endeavor, seeking redemption and restoration, will gratefully find both. In a world where winning appearances are everything, we would do well to remember what is recorded in Matthew 20:16: "So the last will be first, and the first last."

Keys to Kingdom Living: His kingdom, never of this world, is cloaked in humility.

Doorpost: "Jesus found a young donkey and sat on it, just as it is written: Fear no more, Daughter Zion. Look, your King is coming, sitting on a donkey's colt." John 12:14–15

VALUABLE LESSONS FROM CREATION:
A ROOSTER'S REMINDER

*I*n the 1995 movie *Babe*, when a farm couple buys an alarm clock, a resident duck refers to the preposterous gadget as a mechanical rooster. For anyone who's never spent a night on a farm or in the country, roosters crow just before, or at the crack of, dawn. Roosters also crow when a new light source appears.

A rooster played a key role in shaping the apostle Peter on the night of Jesus's betrayal. Its prophesied crow shed light on a broken man at a time he would have preferred to remain in the shadows. In the early evening of that fateful day, Jesus gently told Peter that he would deny knowing Him. Peter vehemently argued that he would never do such a thing. Jesus gently told him, as recorded in Matthew 26:34, that in that same evening Peter would deny him three times before the break of dawn.

Later that night, in a crowd huddling in a courtyard near the home of the high priest, Peter denied he knew Jesus when confronted by a servant girl and two other men. As soon as he made his third denial, we read in Luke 22:61 that "the Lord turned and looked straight at Peter. And Peter remembered the word from the the Lord." Imagine how Peter felt as Jesus's eyes stared into his own. What a watershed moment for a man who was the first of the twelve to discern through the Holy Spirit that Jesus was the promised Messiah, as recorded in Matthew 16:16. Thankfully, Peter didn't remain in his state of guilt and remorse.

He repented of his actions and was forgiven by his compassionate Lord, who had proclaimed Peter as the rock on which He would build His church in Matthew 16:18.

We are all thrown into situations where we are torn between our desire for popularity and our obligation to stand up for God's agenda and all that entails. I know when conversations about TV programs and popular music containing objectionable material are brought up, I'm not always keen to explain why I don't watch, listen to, or even know anything about them. That call is much easier than the one some Christians have had to make when someone holds a gun to their head and asks them if they are Christian. Some have paid for their answers with their lives. I would like to think I would say yes to such a question, but at the end of the day such a hard call is, in reality, unimaginable in many ways. We can certainly pray to be stronger in advance, should such a situation ever arise in our lives.

An experiment conducted on roosters sought to determine if they could be tricked into delivering the same kinds of strong crows at times other than at dawn. A group of scientists led by Takashi Yoshimura determined that "[roosters'] internal clocks take precedence over external cues."[1] Peter's denials were the result of Peter following external rather than internal cues. But before we rush to judgment, do our internal compasses take precedence over the external influences of this world? Or do we assimilate a little too neatly into our environs? Fortunately, when we fall short, Jesus is there to help us pick up the pieces, as He did with Peter.

Keys to Kingdom Living: Pray that your internal clock will trump external cues.

Doorpost: "Peter then denied it again. Immediately a rooster crowed." John 18:27

VALUABLE LESSONS FROM CREATION:
SIGNS OF THE DOVE

*D*oves, primarily turtledoves, are mentioned throughout the Bible. They are designated as an animal for atonement and sacrifice. The small bird was a common sacrifice for families of modest means in ancient times who could not afford to sacrifice larger animals. Doves are also known to play pivotal roles in signaling God's presence (particularly that of the Holy Spirit) and were used by God to visually enhance His communication with His people.

The first dove mentioned specifically in the Bible was in Genesis 8 It was the one Noah released after forty days of rain. When the dove first flew out the small window of the ark, it found nowhere to perch, so it returned. After another seven days, Noah again released the dove. It returned in the evening with a freshly plucked olive leaf. Noah waited another seven days and again sent the dove out a third and final time, and it did not return, so Noah knew it was safe to exit the ark.

Turtledoves, in particular, are popular in literature and song and are featured in the popular song "The Twelve Days of Christmas." Though there is some dispute over its origins, theologians believe the song may have been written by English Catholics to help children learn church doctrine. The "two turtledoves" in the song are said to represent the Old and New Testaments of the Bible. Because doves, more often than not, mate for life, it was a common practice for doves to be released at outdoor wedding ceremonies for many years.

In both instances when the dove appeared in the Old and New Testaments, God was building a bridge between Himself and His people. After the wrath of the flood that wiped out an entire people, save Noah and his family, the dove communicated to Noah that it was safe to disembark and begin again to populate the planet. When the spirit of God descended like a dove, lighting on Jesus, as we read in both Matthew 3 and Luke 3, God communicated within earshot of the disciples that He "took delight" in His Son.

Today we often see depictions of doves on altars and on decorative felt banners in church sanctuaries. This image serves as a reminder of the Holy Spirit's presence. We are blessed to live in this post-Pentecost time. (Prior to Pentecost, God had not sent His Holy Spirit to stay with His people.) Today, the Holy Spirit resides in everyone who professes faith in the one true God, accepts Jesus as Messiah and Lord of their life, and is baptized with "water and the Spirit," as we read in John 3:5. What an awesome privilege to be able to tap into that power daily as sons and daughters of the King!

Keys to Kingdom Living: Thank God for the bridges He builds in your life daily.

Doorpost: "After Jesus was baptized, He went up immediately from the water. The heavens suddenly opened for Him, and He saw the Spirit of God descending like a dove and coming down on Him." Matthew 3:16

VALUABLE LESSONS FROM CREATION:
SHEEP AND GOATS

*B*rian M. Howard's endearing children's song "I Just Wanna Be a Sheep" captures the spirit of a child. He says he simply wants to belong to God's flock and not be lumped in with the goats that won't be welcome in God's kingdom. Christian adults would do well to heed the call to the same right-hand side where Jesus will gather His precious lambs.

The parable of the sheep and the goats in Matthew 25 pivots the gentle, quiet, innocent sheep against the rebellious goats, sometimes mentioned in the Bible as a symbol of evil. There we read that, on judgment day, "All the nations will be gathered before Him, and He will separate them one from another, just as a shepherd separates the sheep from the goats" (Matthew 25:32).

Interestingly enough, there are striking differences in the temperaments of both animals amid many similarities. Sheep instinctively flock and tend to become anxious or even agitated if separated from the rest of the flock. Sheep are easier to fence in than goats, which tend to be more independent than sheep. Historically, sheep are mentioned in the Bible more than 500 times and far more than any other animal, according to the website sheep101.info.

I think the parable of sheep and goats also illustrates the principle of being called to be different in a sea of sameness. Sheep and goats, like Christians and non-Christians, represent all human beings. Both possess a beating heart and bleed red blood. Both

Christians and non-Christians are expected to live 78.8 years on average (in America). You might not be able to tell just by looking at a person whether or not they are a Christ-follower, but Jesus knows. In John 10:14 He identifies Himself as the "good shepherd. I know My own sheep, and they know Me." He goes on to say that He lays down His life for the sheep. He even makes reference to the sheep that are "not of this fold; I must bring them also, and they will listen to My voice. Then there will be one flock, one shepherd" (John 10:16). Jesus refers to the Gentiles here who were grafted into God's plan after the Jews initially rejected Jesus.

The notion of universalism—that all human beings, regardless of their stance on Christ, will ultimately be restored to a right relationship in heaven and in the New Jerusalem—refutes the need for separation. But to embrace that notion means denying the truths Christ taught in this parable, as well as many others. Verses like John 12:32, which reads, "As for Me, if I am lifted up from the earth I will draw all people to Myself," illustrates truths found in Colossians 1:20. There we read that God will reconcile all things unto Himself, compelling the need for further thinking. But what of the lake of fire and the hell mentioned throughout the Bible? The Good Shepherd's love and eternal devotion await both lambs and those currently in the goat herd. The only difference lies in whether they accept the free gift of salvation—or don't.

Keys to Kingdom Living: Cultivate a sheep-like spirit and avoid the goat herd.

Doorpost: "He will put the sheep on His right and the goats on the left." Matthew 25:33

WEEK 7: CONTEMPLATING THE AWE OF GOD

CONTEMPLATING THE AWE OF GOD: HIS DAZZLING CREATION

*a*t the breathtaking sight of a double rainbow, a clear black sky full of sparkling stars, or the birth of a child, many have said they've seen God's amazing handiwork. Of course, there are those who try to explain away the idea of a Divine Architect. But for those touched by faith and the Holy Spirit, many a holy moment has been spent standing in awe of all that God has made.

The astounding variety of plant and animal life on our planet staggers the mind. From the tall redwood to the bonsai, the tiny lily of the valley blossom and the largesse of the bird of paradise, God's trees and blooms dazzle both countryside and coffee table. The kinetic pattern of the zebra bears sharp contrast to the camouflaging skill of the gecko. The fluffy Himalayan cat beckons to be petted, while the sight of a porcupine's prickly exterior may send you running for the hills. For the faith-filled eye, it's easy to give creation credit where credit is due. Yet creation skeptics persist in explaining away how everything came to be, despite compelling evidence of a divine order.

It is "well with our soul" when we continually praise God for the wondrous world He has made. Whenever we inhale the scent of a blooming peony, taste the exploding juices of a robust cherry tomato, feel the gritty sand of a summer shoreline, hear the coo of a dove greeting the morning sun, or feast our eyes on a lunar eclipse, we can shoot God an arrow prayer of thanks for His divine design and its exquisite execution.

The sheer amazement prompted by creation was the inspiration for many Bible verses, including Romans 1:20 which reminds us, "Ever since the creation of the world His eternal power and divine nature, invisible though they are, have been understood and seen through the things He has made." Paul wrote this to illustrate that men who've not directly received the good news of Jesus Christ have still been privy to God's greatness through exposure to all He's made.

Like many parents before and after me, no moment in my life clarifies more succinctly for me that God is the Giver of Life more than when my oldest son was born. Because he was adopted and I didn't give birth to him, it was very clear to me that he was literally a gift from God. Observing his little seed-pearl fingernails, hearing his little-lamb cry, and taking in the precious aroma of his silky newborn hair left me breathless when I contemplated each in its entirety. Sorry, *Big Bang Theory*, you'll never be more than a television show to me. God made the world in six days, and He was more than a little right in saying "it was good."

Keys to Kingdom Living: Stop not only to smell the roses but to thank God for them.

Doorpost: "Ask the animals, and they will instruct you; ask the birds of the sky, and they will tell you. Or speak to the earth, and it will instruct you; let the fish of the sea inform you. Which of these does not know that the hand of the LORD has done this?" Job 12:7–9

CONTEMPLATING THE AWE OF GOD:
THE RAINBOW

*I*t's almost impossible for us to comprehend the impact of Noah's unfathomable report of an impending flood to a community of people who'd never seen one drop of rain. Up until the time of Noah, we are told in Genesis 2 that the Lord "had not made it rain on the land. . . . But water would come out of the ground and water the entire surface of the land" (v. 5–6). We are told later that, indeed, waters covered the earth for forty days and forty nights until Noah saw the tops of the mountains. After Noah built an altar and prepared sacrifices pleasing to the Lord, the Lord made a covenant with Noah and future generations never to "strike down every living thing" as He had done (Genesis 8:21). He went on to say that He would never again send a flood to destroy the earth.

As a visible and recurring sign of this covenant, God fashioned the most colorful, most miraculous art project in the history of the world: the rainbow. Who hasn't had their breath taken away at the sight of a rainbow across a dark sky after a rain, in that brief moment between torrential rain and reappearing sunshine? Whether viewed as a small half-arc, in a left-to-right single sweep, or in tandem as a dazzling duo, few natural sights are more colorful or more significant to God's people.

Of course, science loves to explain the rainbow as a purely meteorological phenomenon caused by the reflection, refraction, and dispersion of light in water droplets working together to form the colorful arc. The rainbow might be a full circle, but we are only privy to an aboveground view. Naturally, for God's people, the rainbow is more than a mere photo op or a page out of a science textbook. For us, the rainbow stands out as a visible covenant in a precious handful of unseen, though equally powerful, promises from God. While faith may be required to accept the purpose of the rainbow, it isn't required to simply view it.

God, the consummate artist, working in the mediums of water and light created on the first and second days of creation, fashioned a living sculpture that cannot be approached, touched, or preserved. Though the human eye may only see basic shades of red, orange, yellow, green, blue, indigo, and violet, there are one hundred distinct hues in God's magnificent *objet d'art*. Talk about a vast color palette! People have tried to attach man-made legends of leprechauns and pots of gold that are supposedly waiting at every rainbow's end. But the treasure of the rainbow is not as destination but in destiny. It was the beginning of God's plan to preserve rather than destroy His people.

A rainbow sighting for me also generates a more personal response. When I see a rainbow in the sky, it reminds me that before I even knew Him, God rescued me from the storm that was my life and made something beautiful out of my ashes.

Keys to Kingdom Living: Rainbows are visible reminders of God's covenant with us.

Doorpost: "I have placed My bow in the clouds, and it will be a sign of the covenant between Me and the earth." Genesis 9:13

CONTEMPLATING THE AWE OF GOD:
SEAS, WALKING ON LIFE'S SEAS

ew earthly things are as unfathomable as what lies beneath the sea. As non-amphibians, we can only go so deep beneath the surface of the water, and for so long. And with oceans covering 71 percent of the earth, it's safe to say most of the world remains a deep mystery to us. So the idea of gliding across the surface of the water or walking on the ocean floor with two parted-water curtains on either side of us as we saunter about sounds implausible at the very least . . . and terrifying at its worst.

Yet when we look at the procession of the ancient Israelites and the short walk of Peter, we see evidence of what our amazing God is capable of bringing to pass.

When God makes a way to rescue His chosen people from captivity, He instructs Moses to lead the people most literally through the Red Sea as He parts it. We read in Exodus 14 how the Lord instructed Moses to stretch out his hand over the sea as God drove it back "with a powerful east wind . . . and turned the sea into dry land" (v. 21). Once the waters were divided for a path, with walls on the left and right of the ocean bed, the Israelites went through the sea on dry ground (v. 22).

The amazing sight of this miraculous event cannot be underestimated, no matter how many times we've viewed a recreated form of it in the Cecil B. DeMille film *The Ten Commandments*. It's a metaphor for how God wants to lead us though seemingly impossible circumstances. He wants us to trust Him as He leads us on a journey that seems impossible to complete, yet He wants us to trust him through it. What could be a more daunting earthly sight in nature than an anti-gravitational mass of water?

Another water walk is recorded in Matthew 14. The disciples had gone into a boat on the lake as Jesus had instructed while He went up a mountainside to pray. Later than night, as a storm kicked around the waves, Jesus walked on the lake toward the boat. When Peter saw his Lord, he said, "Lord, if it's You, command me to come to You on the water" (v. 28). When Jesus told him to come, Peter walked out onto the water toward Jesus. But when he saw the wind, he cried out in fear for Jesus to save him, which He did. We read in verse 33 that the awestruck disciples worshipped Him afterwards.

Having read these stories over and over, it's conceivable our awe may get lost in their familiarity. Do we really stop to ponder God's awe as we should? It turns out awe is more than just good for our own souls. University of California, Berkeley professor Dacher Keltner concluded that awe is the "ultimate 'collective emotion.'"[1] He believes it motivates people to do things that enhance the greater good. He found that awe helps shift focus from "narrow self-interest to the interests of the group to which we belong."[2] Berkeley lab experiments revealed those who experienced more awe cooperated more, shared more resources, and sacrificed more for others than their more jaded counterparts, just as Jesus did.

Keys to Kingdom Living: Keep your awe of God's incomparable character alive.

Doorpost: "God, You are awe-inspiring in Your sanctuaries." Psalm 68:35

CONTEMPLATING THE AWE OF GOD: CONTROLLING CHAOS IN THE TOWER OF BABEL

*T*ime after time, God has been compelled to save mankind from himself. One of the instances of this benevolent behavior occurs in Genesis 11. Here we read of the people's desire to construct a city and a tower "with its top in the sky" (v. 4), as if to attempt to invade God's lofty territory in their self-elevated arrogance. Up until this point, men only had one language, and communication was easily achieved from tribe to tribe. As God saw His people trying to make a name for themselves, as is recorded in Genesis 11:4, we see how their pride trumps everything. Even in this, the remnant that God preserved after the great flood, trouble and sin nature returned.

In the middle of this foolish build, God recognized that it was only the beginning of what they could do. And "nothing they plan to do will be impossible for them" (Genesis 11:6). So He decided He would confuse their language, so that they wouldn't understand one another's speech (v. 7). With one heavenly notion and a wave of His mighty hand, God confused the language of the entire earth from community to community. He also "scattered them over the face of the whole earth," as is recorded in verse 8. Even today, when language is not easily understood, it is referred to as "babble," a noun hearkening back to the tower of that same name: Babel.

Only the universe's Creator could change its audible and geographical makeup with the wave of a hand. Talk about awe-inspiring. Imagine what kind of a scene it must have been, witnessing the complete change of the face of the earth and the undermining of foolish and dangerous plans. We aren't told in Scripture what reaction the people had except that they ceased building the tower and they were scattered across the earth. Someone might have been up in the tower one minute and on a mountaintop in Alaska the next! Or a guy might have been on the ground talking to a fellow builder only to see confusion on the face of the intended recipient who didn't understand a word his friend said. Of course we have no way of knowing precisely what happened, but it's an intriguing exercise to try to imagine.

The people who dreamed and worked on the tower had lost their awe of God. Instead, they cultivated an awe relegated to their own abilities and gifts that God had actually given them. The tower itself, seemingly gigantic to earthly inhabitants, is so small from a divine standpoint that God had to exit heaven to come down and see it, as we read in Genesis 11:5. When the creation confuses its greatness with the Creator, trouble is sure to follow. Thankfully, God always has the best interests of His people at heart, just as He does for you and me. And what might feel enormous to us pales in comparison to his divine undertakings.

I can't begin to count the number of times God has saved me from myself. If I don't keep my pride in check, I often find myself attempting some version of ill-conceived worship at the Tower of Me. But when I stay rooted in God's word, I remain mindful of just how awesome God Almighty, the maker of heaven and earth, really is.

Keys to Kingdom Living: We should worship God and not make idols of ourselves or out of anything we make.

Doorpost: "The LORD will fight for you; you must be quiet." Exodus 14:14

CONTEMPLATING THE AWE OF GOD: THE VIRGIN BIRTH

*H*umans, even those belonging to God, aren't always mindful of the power behind life's everyday miracles. The rising and setting of the sun or the conception and birth of another human being aren't any less amazing because of their frequency. Even with helpful reminders such as Psalm 139:13 in which David speaks of God knitting him together in his mother's womb, sometimes we humans want to take all the credit for making babies. But the rain dance doesn't bring the rain, and even physical acts of passion alone do not a baby make. The miracle of human life between a man and a woman remains a hallmark of God's handiwork, no matter who tries to take the credit.

Certainly, the unique conception of the Christ child is unequivocally divinely inspired and orchestrated by the one true God alone. Though Mary herself couldn't begin to understand how such a miraculous thing could come to pass inside of her, she believed and trusted God during the process. Even today, some who study the Bible struggle with this fact, despite the heavy documentation found in the gospels as well as a foretelling in Isaiah 7:14.

When it comes to arts and crafts, creativity always relies on supplies and materials in order to transform random objects into thoughtful creations. I remember thinking smugly to myself when I was younger that a writer's creations don't require materials. Pen and paper or a keyboard and a printer are nice luxuries, but I justified that oral recitation doesn't require any gear. But as I pondered it further, I realized that without my God-given brain to formulate, as well as my tongue to speak those thoughts, my creations would cease to exist. In fact, we read in Acts 17:28 that "in Him we live and move and exist." That pretty much sums up our contributions versus the kinds of amazing things God can do.

The more we understand God's character, the more we realize that only God Himself can make something out of nothing. He didn't have a supply list to procure. When he first formed Adam out of the dust of the earth, He began with dust He first created. When God went about creating the promised Messiah, He could have created something without involving anyone else. But instead, He included—but did not rely on—a faithful follower of God, a pure virgin with a servant's heart for obedience. Mary exhibited a willingness to sacrifice herself on a number of levels to play a part in orchestrating His perfect plan. We read of her humble response in Luke 1. God's selection of her didn't cause her to become puffed up or to take bows or give an acceptance speech. She simply declared herself as a servant of the Lord (v. 38).

Are your "creations" fashioned to bring you accolades that belong to God? Make an honest inventory of motives, making sure that your awe of God's mighty power is at the forefront of all you undertake. Keep in mind this helpful reminder from Paul that "whatever you do, do everything for God's glory" (1 Corinthians 10:31).

Keys to Kingdom Living: God's inimitable mighty power is the ultimate life source.

Doorpost: "The virgin will become pregnant and give birth to a son, and they will name Him Immanuel, which is translated 'God is with us.'" Matthew 1:23

CONTEMPLATING THE AWE OF GOD: MULTIPLYING BREAD AND FISH

The he miracle of Jesus multiplying the five loaves and two fish offers a wealth of valuable lessons about generosity, obedience, responsibility, conservation, and redistribution. But the amazing tale of this decidedly meager offering from a small boy in the hands of a really big God deserves to be appreciated for its triumph over improbability and its indisputable "wow factor."

Imagine witnessing this amazing miracle: the feeding of thousands of people out in the middle of nowhere with supplies that would fit into the palms of two hands. No matter how many times this scene has been captured on film, I don't think we can fully imagine what the experience was like for those who were there. Imagine the incredible quality of bread and fish made by God Himself, the texture, aroma, and taste. Surely it was like nothing else they'd ever tasted, even though we don't get those kinds of details.

This sort of miracle is the kind of thing God specializes in. He loves to demonstrate His divine power in the middle of seemingly impossible circumstances. He uses regular people with willing servants' hearts. He even uses murderers such as Moses, Paul, and David, and prostitutes like Rahab, to accomplish his work. He wants the people who are willing to be used by Him to sacrifice their resources and time to accomplish His work.

I still remember the words of my young son after he spent a year bringing his offering to Sunday school: "What does Jesus do with my quarters?" In his mind, a few quarters wouldn't amount to making much of a difference in a world where thousands are starving. Yet over time, after participating in our church school's offering program, which I started based on his comment, he came to understand the importance of his giving and cultivated a generous and loving heart as a result of his participation.

Our resources and time offerings might seem like drops in the bucket to us. But giving is like voting: if everyone doesn't participate, the system collapses and its impact is largely diminished. The quarters from the offering program, over time, turned into thousands of dollars at my son's school. And what a boy's mom allotted for a single lunch, he surrendered to Jesus. That lunch ended up feeding over five thousand people, Afterwards, twelve baskets of pieces of bread and fish were left over.

What are you holding onto that might seem like a meager offering that God could use for His glory? Are you gripping too tightly to your schedule, your earnings, or your possessions? What stands between miracles God is poised to do and your willingness to sacrifice can sometimes make a significant difference to His kingdom work outcome. Join me in partnering with God to bring about all that He desires to accomplish through us.

Keys to Kingdom Living: Partner with God in joy and humility as you give, thanking Him in advance for how He will multiply your offering.

Doorpost: "He took the seven loaves and the fish, and He gave thanks, broke them, and kept on giving them to the disciples, and the disciples gave them to the crowds. They all ate and were filled." Matthew 15:36–37

CONTEMPLATING THE AWE OF GOD: RESURRECTION FROM THE DEAD

ales of doctors restarting a heart or reviving a patient on an operating table are the stuff of newspaper articles and medical journals. Tales from attending physicians of people who have moved into the light but were somehow called back to this side of life are part of a hot genre of nonfiction offerings at bookstores around the country. In reality, mortality's outcome is not merely reliant on skilled medical professionals. So then, who remains the final authority when someone lives or dies? It is the Giver of Life. He is also the Sustainer of it and the only one capable of resurrecting it. Though He may call upon His hands and feet sometimes, and weave their input and handiwork to accomplish His will, He remains in full control.

It doesn't take a genius to acknowledge that everyone who walks this earth has an expiration date this side of eternity. The old "death and taxes" cliché reminds us of the only two sure things to be counted on in this life. But in rare cases, miraculous resurrections have occurred, all fueled by God power. During Jesus's ministry on the earth, He raised the widow of Nain's daughter (Luke 7:11–16), the twelve-year-old daughter (Mark 5:35–43), and His friend Lazarus (John 11:1–44). Of course the most monumental resurrection that changed the course of human history for all eternity was the resurrection of Jesus Himself. He permanently conquered death for Himself as well as for all who believe in Him.

Wrapping our heads around this resurrection truth is no easy task. Naturally, as Christians, we accept the resurrection at face value, engaging our muscles of faith to help us arrive at a place of acceptance. Of course, there are many atheists and skeptics who vehemently question the validity of resurrection. Yet no other major religious leader has ever made this claim. None were crucified in front of impartial witnesses, laid in a guarded and sealed tomb, only to rise three days later and appear to many individuals. Among some of the so-called gods of our day—Muhammad, Krishna, Buddha, and Confucius—not one of them boasts accomplishing such a stunning feat.

How awesome it must have been for the relatives of the two girls and Jesus's friend to be reunited with those they'd lost in what surely seemed like a permanent and final separation. As for the disciples, who had once walked away from everything, they had to wonder—for three days, at a minimum, while Jesus remained in the tomb—if their years with Jesus had been a waste of their time. Seeing Jesus reappear to them must have been mind-blowing. Yet in our familiarity with this story, we can become complacent in our reaction.

We need to continually remind ourselves of what an incredible present the Giver of Life bestowed on His undeserving people whom He redeemed and made new. He sacrificed His Son to rescue us from death and set us on a path of everlasting life, a God-sized task that only He could ever accomplish. And it's one that changed our eternal destiny forever. Talk about a vault-worthy treasure!

Keys to Kingdom Living: Only the one true God is capable of raising the dead to life.

Doorpost: "I am the resurrection and the life." John 11:25

WEEK 8: NOT-SO-LITTLE THINGS TO LOCK UP

NOT-SO-LITTLE THINGS TO LOCK UP:
A COMMENT IN PASSING

*O*ften when we hear the term *evangelism*, we envision long-term campaigns to bring people to Jesus. Certainly, formal strategies regarding approach, events, or methods are used to spark interest on the part of friends needing to hear about Jesus. But sometimes we miss the forest for the trees by overthinking things. While we need to tend to the forest, sometimes we are called to just scatter some seeds with our spare seconds to help win friends for Christ.

We need to optimize our effectiveness for God by using all our time wisely. We daydream or dive into our cell phone in spare moments, missing the opportunity to comfort the frazzled mom with the toddler in the checkout line or compliment the smartly dressed elderly widow who hasn't spoken to a soul all day.

Are we more inclined to ignore or engage in the situations calling for a passing comment? They may make a real difference in a person's outlook. A friend I know prays daily in her morning quiet time for God to bring her just these kinds of opportunities for connection. She prays that she will not only recognize them when they occur but optimize these moments for the glory of God and to the best of her ability.

Such a prayer does more than just increase her mindfulness; it also increases her effectiveness. It requires her to make a counter-cultural change in the way she lives her life and keeps her schedule. But she is quick to say that it's entirely possible that her investments will pay unimaginable dividends in this life and, more importantly, the next. She imagines more divine appointments in heaven where she's likely to learn of the collective difference made by the sum total of her passing comments. Ironically, though she doesn't appear organized, she maximizes such moments and plants an enormous number of seeds.

Aside from the passing comments we can make in person, it's also possible to widen our sphere of influence through the use of social media. Perusing your social media feed to reach out to the person having a bad day, or struggling with a long-term health problem or family dilemma. Doing so may bring someone one step closer to exiting their pit of despair. A kind word, a Bible verse (even without the scriptural "address") can inspire and spur someone on to good deeds of their own, as we read in Hebrews 10:24.

Of course, it would be naïve to think that all passing comments are welcomed and appreciated. Jesus warned us that some of the seeds we scatter are sure to fall on rocky soil. But that should never deter us from keeping our hand in the seed bag, always ready to toss another handful in the hopes that some will joyfully take root.

Keys to Kingdom Living: Spending the currency of spare moments by investing in people who need encouragement is a great way to brighten someone's day and store up treasures in heaven.

Doorpost: "She opens her mouth with wisdom and loving instruction is on her tongue." Proverbs 31:26

NOT-SO-LITTLE THINGS TO LOCK UP:
A LOVING TOUCH

$\mathcal{T}$he pastor of my church often encourages his flock to actively hug, as is his personal custom. He says he particularly encourages the hugging of the elderly, who enjoy smaller social circles than their younger counterparts. Though there are thousands in his congregation, he's often found making the rounds with his famous bear hugs before he delivers his sermons whenever the opportunity safely presents itself.

General physical touch is experiencing a sharp decline. During the COVID-19 pandemic, it's been nearly impossible to experience it with anyone not living directly under your roof. Yet while it may be underrated by some, its importance is well documented. In society at large today, where an implied hands-off policy is the order of the day, hugs are endangered. This endangered status is taking a toll on people of all ages, due in part to an increasingly dehumanized society where electronic communication replaces face-to-face conversation and circumvents opportunities for physical human interaction.

We are living in a drought of physical contact which *Psychology Today* magazine calls "skin hunger."[1] Research shows that babies who are not held and nuzzled enough will literally stop growing and, even with proper nutrition, will die of touch starvation.[2] Orphanage infant mortality rates of 30 to 40 percent bear out the findings.[3]

The dearth of general touch in society today bears sharp

contrast to the uptick in sexual hookups. Casual sex doesn't compare to the intentionally loving touch. In fact, some studies show that lack of loving touch in childhood results in a higher level of promiscuity. In Gary Chapman's bestselling book *The Five Love Languages*, physical touch is listed as one of the five primary ways individuals need genuine love shown to them. Chapman, like others who have written and spoken about the importance of touch, say it's a mistake to limit its importance exclusively to the sexual realm.

Purely loving touches are vital to our well-being. They help us feel connected to others, ground us by providing much-needed sensory stimulation, promote bonding and trust, and have even been found to lower blood pressure. Crime statistics show that cultures lavishing more affection on infants and children produce adult citizens less prone to crimes of violence.

Jesus understood the power of physical touch and always made it a point to lay His hands on people who were considered highly untouchable, including the leper on the mountain (Matthew 8:1–3) and the blind man near Siloam who was thought to be cursed (John 9:6–34). When we touch the homeless person who hasn't had a fresh bath for a number of days, we become more like Jesus. I remember encountering a bleeding Rwandan who'd had a bike accident on the side of the road on the last day of a mission trip. Our plastic glove supply depleted, and in the midst of the AIDS crisis, our team initially paused but eventually rolled up its sleeves to help. It's what Jesus would have done.

Keys to Kingdom Living: Offer a hug or high five to express Christ-like love whenever reasonable and possible.

Doorpost: "Then the one with human likeness touched me again and strengthened me." Daniel 10:18

NOT-SO-LITTLE THINGS TO LOCK UP:
A MOMENT OF YOUR TIME

*W*hen people told time with ancient sundials, they were completely unconcerned with charting the seconds or even minutes between the hours the device was created to measure. As timekeeping has become more sophisticated, its accuracy has improved—but the way time is spent has not necessarily followed suit. How ironic!

Today's stopwatches record the milliseconds that delineate the difference between gold and silver medals. Video gaming conquests ride on the times of competing warriors. *Jeopardy* contestants scribble their FINAL JEOPARDY! answers as the show's official "Think" soundtrack ticks off the thirty precious seconds allotted for answering. Teenagers around the world are "living and dying" during the seconds they wait between text message responses.

In our microwave society where "instant" is king, how all of our "found" minutes are being spent is a million-dollar question. Are we taking time to help a friend with a problem, or are we frittering away the hours playing Words with Friends on our cell phones? Are we using the hours that might have been spent lovingly preparing a slow-cooked meal streaming trash TV until our eyes are bloodshot? Or are we using all our free time to catch up on work, ignoring the needs of those we love by investing in a workplace that can't and won't ever love us back?

It's important to make space to spend wisely the little moments between the red ink items on our calendars. Such wise expenditures include seemingly unimportant transactions such as listening to a joke your child eagerly wants to relay, or fully attending to a friend's long health update that may contain one too many details for your personal taste. Investing time into your relationships is important, but it isn't just your loved ones you should be investing in. Helping the elderly load groceries into their car in a parking lot, bringing your sick neighbor's trash cans up from the curb, or returning the friendly banter of a shopper in line with you at the store—these small kindnesses not only bless the recipient, they keep your mindfulness attuned to the needs of others rather than your own.

During a family outing a while back, our excellent service prompted me to comment that our server was a shoo-in for a "best waitress" contest. Weeks later, at the same restaurant, she told us she'd experienced the death of a close friend. Barely able to contain her tears, she continued to provide us with excellent service. We took time to offer her compassion and listen to her story, even though our family rarely gets together. We offered to pray for her, an act she genuinely appreciated. Later, she bought us dessert and thanked us for caring. Sometimes little things make a big difference.

Keys to Kingdom Living: Be a good steward with your time currency.

Doorpost: "All my days were written in Your book and planned before a single one of them began." Psalm 139:16

NOT-SO-LITTLE THINGS TO LOCK UP:
SMALL RESPONSES TO CRISIS

*S*ometimes when the world is crashing down around someone, our first response is to jump to the conclusion that if we can't solve the person's entire problem, the best thing to do is to turn our heads. We pretend as if we are clueless to their problems or steer clear of any intervention.

To be sure, the godly response to any crisis is best determined by a leading from the Lord. But sometimes selfishness prohibits us from taking even a small part in responding to someone else's pain. Certainly, responses for close friends and family members would be more self-sacrificial than those made for a complete stranger. But, like the Good Samaritan, we are also called to help our neighbors and the people we come into contact with in our communities and even beyond.

When someone I know, or even don't know, experiences a crisis, and I witness or read or hear about it, I shouldn't bury my head in the sand like an ostrich—even if that is a tempting game plan. In that moment when a crisis is in front of us, we can send an arrow prayer and ask God to direct us on how to make a difference in the situation.

On a recent trip to France, my girlfriends and I were checking in for our flight when a fellow passenger began to have a seizure. One of my friends, who happened to be a doctor, tended to her immediate medical needs until airport medical staff could arrive. As the rest of us stood by, we began to pray among, ourselves for the woman. Suddenly, there was a small opening in the crowded circle around her, and the physical opening prompted a leading from the Holy Spirit. My friend had a Bible she had brought on the trip to give away, but she had yet to part with it. I told her I thought this was the opportunity she'd been waiting for. She handed it to me, and I walked it over to her circle of relatives. They were kneeling, paralyzed in fear over their convulsing loved one. I remember being a bit afraid that I might be interfering, but I felt led to proceed anyway. I handed the woman's British sister the small Bible, and she gratefully clutched it as I told her we were praying for her. She smiled, and I put my hand briefly on her shoulder before moving quietly away from the chaos.

Though the interaction took but a minute, I believe it meant something to the family. They expressed their gratitude as they moved from the gate to a more private area. Making even small efforts in crises glorifies God when motivations are pure and the Spirit leads. Even if strangers are the beneficiaries, small yet effective ways to bring our Christian love present themselves. Only God knows whether or not such kindnesses might lead someone a smidge closer to salvation.

Keys to Kingdom Living: Pray for divine guidance for ways to act as Jesus's hands and feet in crisis.

Doorpost: "But you will receive power when the Holy Spirit has come on you, and you will be My witnesses." Acts 1:8

NOT-SO-LITTLE THINGS TO LOCK UP:
A WORD OF HOPE

*T*he stray moments spent in the store checkout once spent chatting with fellow shoppers are now being redirected to our phones. With an increase in online shopping, we can leave the house less often than was once necessary. This phenomenon is isolating us from community in big and small ways. I'm guilty of this as well, but of late I'm making a concerted effort to put down my device and observe my neighbors to see who might need an encouraging intervention.

Encouragement, considered a spiritual gift, is an investment that costs nothing to give yet pays enormous dividends. It can come in the form of a single sentence in a casual public setting, be offered in a friendly telephone conversation, or reinforced over and over during something as simple as a morning coffee. It may be a one-time occurrence with a stranger or a part of your daily vernacular conversations with your spouse, child, or friend.

The Lord has pressed it into my heart to care for widows and orphans, as we are told to do in James 1:27. As well as sponsoring students in third world countries, I try to make a point of checking in with ladies I know who have lost their husbands due to death or divorce. My goal is to help alleviate the isolation that comes with being uncoupled. I also try to compliment them when they look nice in a society where youth is revered to sad extremes. I'm learning as I age that it is easy to feel invisible or even marginalized in our youth-oriented society. In recent years I have become more aware of how important it is to encourage third-world orphans not only through financial support but also by the care that is communicated through "attaboys." This kind of verbal support lets them know someone on this earth cares about them and believes in them. A teen may read Jeremiah 29:11 and intellectualize that God has plans and purposes. But when a Christian acting as "Jesus with skin on" encourages them with God's promises and provides support in conjunction with it, such words of hope and the practical expressions of it go a long way.

Jesus often encouraged His disciples as well as those He spoke to individually and in groups. To the downtrodden, He said, "Come to Me, all of you who are weary and burdened, and I will give you rest" (Matthew 11:28). To those drowning in challenging circumstances, He said, "Be courageous! I have conquered the world" (John 16:33). To people who have lost their hope, Jesus encourages them to keep asking, keep searching, and keep knocking because "everyone who asks receives, and the one who searches finds, and to the one that knocks, the door will be opened" (Matthew 7:7–8). To the disciples confounded at the appearance of their risen Lord, He said in John 14:27, "Peace I leave with you ... Your heart must not be troubled or fearful."

Keys to Kingdom Living: Little words of hope go a long way for a friend or stranger.

Doorpost: "And let us be concerned about one another in order to promote love and good works ... encouraging each other, and all the more as you see the day drawing near." Hebrews 10:24–25

NOT-SO-LITTLE THINGS TO LOCK UP:
A SMALL TOKEN

I once had a friend of great means. When it came time to try to buy her something for Christmas or for her birthday, I would stress about what I could possibly give her that she did not already have. One day, I made a joke about this, and she proceeded to pull out a book. Inside it was a plain paper bookmark with stickers of dogs and the name of her dog written onto it. She told me it was one of her favorite things. It was something I had made her for less than a dollar a few years earlier.

We don't need to break the bank to offer a small token. Likewise, when small tokens are offered, especially from strangers, we should delight even more in receiving them. Once while I was window-shopping in London, a British woman tapped me on the shoulder and asked me if I would like to have a bouquet of fragrant lilies. I must admit that initially I was kind of suspicious what the catch might be, but then she told me that she wasn't going straight home, so instead of lugging them around, she wanted to give them away. I thanked her and took them back to our hotel where we thoroughly enjoyed them for many days. I've thought from time to time about this spontaneous gift and hope she knew what joy it brought me.

Sometimes tokens can be more thought-out to increase their effectiveness. I know someone who carries around small plastic bag packets for the homeless. They include practical things such as dried fruits and nuts as well as soap and some encouraging leaflet-style Christian books that cost a couple of bucks at our church bookstore. This well-thought-out token not only meets their needs but will be used for the intended purpose, unlike cash. Money is sometimes a less-effective provision, particularly for people struggling with addictions who might be tempted to spend it on drugs or alcohol. She keeps these packs in her car so she is ready to respond to a person with a sign or someone she might see in a parking lot asking for assistance.

Of course, a token is only good if it's distributed. We can carry around dozens of five-dollar gift cards for inexpensive meals, but if we don't pass them out, what good will they do? We need to cultivate mindfulness when it comes to people in need. Instead of saying to ourselves that if we can't give hundreds of dollars to something, why bother to give anyway, we need to respond here and there when a moment arises with a small gesture at the very least, working our way up to something more substantial if God calls us to it.

Some Bible scholars have suggested that the image of Jesus on the cross with His hands nailed to it and His feet bound serve as a reminder of this principle. With the completion of His death, and until He comes again in glory, Jesus is literally relying on our hands and feet to bring the good news to this broken world. A token may be a great starting point to a more impactful end game in bringing the good news. But it's only effective if we circulate that currency.

Keys to Kingdom Living: Giving little things reflects your Christ-like compassion, serving as a springboard from which you can share your joy and hope.

Doorpost: "A gift opens doors for a man and brings him before the great." Proverbs 18:16

NOT-SO-LITTLE THINGS TO LOCK UP:
A QUICK JOT

*W*ho doesn't treasure a handwritten card or note amidst the sea of junk circulars that fill our mailboxes? And in the age of the text, where words disappear without a trace, isn't it nice to celebrate a more permanent form of communiqué?

When it comes to throwing away cards and notes, I am hopeless. Scouts for the show *Hoarders* would find a veritable treasure trove of notes from family members and friends that I cannot bear to discard. I hold onto Christmas cards for two years, and even then I don't throw all of them away—I donate them to crafty girls I know who transform them into encore works of art. I have a bulletin board full of encouraging notes I've collected over the years from a variety of people, written to me by teachers, parents, friends, and my oldest son. I doubt I will ever be able to throw those away.

I'm probably not alone in my love of receiving notes, but I also love giving them. Though many people gravitate toward a schedule for their jots, waiting until a prominent holiday or a crisis, I send unexpected notes to brighten someone's day almost out of the blue. I keep a card box handy with a variety of all-occasion cards as well as those for more specific needs, along with special postage stamps and inexpensive stickers to help my correspondence stand out. But those details aren't important; a note written on lined paper can speak volumes when it's written from the heart. On all my notes, I try to jot down a pertinent Bible verse that speaks to the occasion. If the person is a nonbeliever, I sometimes just include the sentiment without the reference so that particular truth may be more well-received.

I remember a while back, a woman in my Bible study group shared her desire to start a small study group of her own. She shared honestly about her fears that she wasn't qualified enough. This woman, who had been studying the Bible for decades, simply needed some encouragement. I acted on a leading from God and went to the Christian bookstore to find just the right card to encourage her. The following week at the regular study time, she thanked me for the card and said how much it meant to her.

A quick jot on someone's social media feed can also brighten their day, even if that person is a friend of a friend you don't know. A quick "praying for you" lets them know someone cares. (Of course, you'll need to take a moment to follow through with that prayer.) Kind words can greatly encourage the troubled or isolated.

Perhaps the best examples of notes of encouragement in the Bible come from Paul. He was constantly writing to congregations in Corinth, Philippi, Galatia, Colossea, and Rome. He also wrote to Timothy, whom he mentored, and offered specific encouragement regarding spiritual gifts that continues to inspire Christians. We, too, can follow suit and bless others in our lives today.

Keys to Kingdom Living: Even short notes to others can encourage in lasting ways.

Doorpost: "Write down this vision; clearly inscribe it on tablets." Habakkuk 2:2

WEEK 9: THE TREASURED GIFT OF LISTENING

THE TREASURED GIFT OF LISTENING:
TO GOD IN THE QUIET MOMENTS

On a recent trip to Provence, our group of four stumbled on an amazing image in the French countryside. The sun peeked through violet clouds, struggling to emit pink and orange rays as the day was drawing to a close and rain was attempting to break through. We spotted a long gravel driveway lined with fragrant, recently manicured lavender bushes. Green cypress trees lined the walkway of a gorgeous chateau. Grapevines with bright orange-and-red leaves blanketed the surrounding hills. We drove up to the French stone farmhouse and began taking pictures, fully aware that at any moment someone could come out and shoo us away. These shots are so amazingly colorful, and the lighting so unbelievably perfect, that people who've seen them say they look fake.

The most incredible sight of the day, though, was the double rainbow that appeared over the horizon of this already picturesque scene. We stood in awe of its majesty, and I broke away from the group just to be alone with God for a moment of my own. The next morning we were still basking in the memories when the Lord brought Psalm 19 to memory:

> *The heavens declare the glory of God,*
> *and the sky proclaims the work of His hands.*
> *Day after day they pour out speech;*
> *night after night they communicate knowledge.*

There is no speech; there are no words;
their voice is not heard.
Their message has gone out to all the earth,
and their words to the ends of the world. (v. 1–4)

In the world's deafening cacophony of booming car stereos, banal, interruptive talk show banter, and political grandstanding, God can say more with a whispering image from His creation than all of these distractions combined could ever convey. But He won't demand your attention like Donald Trump or Whoopi Goldberg. We need to be tuned to what God is saying to us in the quiet moments. There is a memorable line in a poem by Carl Sandburg that reads, "The fog comes on little cat feet."[1] He implies here that the largesse of fog, which can obstruct entire horizons, mountain ranges, and bridges, does not storm into being, but slowly creeps, changing an entire landscape.

God's communication is like that. The shimmering glow of a full moon, the heady fragrance from an orange tree, the booming rush of a waterfall, the juicy gush from a bite of watermelon, and the smooth feel of a baby's cheek on your palm: all these things are gifts from Him. The glorious seasons, the menagerie of creatures great and small, as well as the crowning jewel of His creation, human beings, are created in His very image. All point to a Creator by whom all things were made, and "in Him we live and move and exist" (Acts 17:28).

People often say they've never heard the audible voice of God, but the truth is He talks to us all day long through His creation. The question is, are we listening?

Keys to Kingdom Living: Take time to savor God's communication through creation.

Doorpost: "All that He does is splendid and majestic." Psalm 111:3

THE TREASURED GIFT OF LISTENING:
TO GOD IN THE WORKPLACE

avigating the waters of bringing "salt and light" to fellow employees in a secular workplace can be a dicey proposition in today's world. In a culture where Christmas trees might be prohibited or religious symbols banned from desktops, sharing Jesus in direct or even indirect ways may violate company policy. When this is the case, it is vital that we discern what God would have us do to make an impact for His kingdom.

A woman in my life group at church once worked for a Fortune 500 company. Their employee handbook strictly prohibited religious symbols of any kind on desktops or in cubicles and offices. It also outlined in stern language that no employee was permitted to share any faith-based beliefs on company property. This included the gifting of books or pamphlets and even applied to casual conversation in the workplace.

One day, one of her regular vendors reached out to her for clarity regarding a business matter. She set aside valuable time to help him, since he shared that his position was in jeopardy. As they wrapped up, he thanked her, saying to her, "I know you are a Christian." Stunned, my friend asked how he knew that, fearing that perhaps she had unwittingly violated the company's policy. He told her it was primarily because she was kind and fair in her business dealings, but he had also noticed in her company bio that she wrote she was "blessed." Her sweet fragrance opened a beautiful dialogue between the two of them. Further, it affirmed my friend's discernment; she had carefully yet effectively brought Jesus into her workplace.

The church needs "fewer cheerleaders and more ambassadors," a friend of mine once said. In my opinion, Jesus emphasized ambassadorship over evangelism, though neither was mutually exclusive. He spoke truth to the woman at the well, to Zacchaeus, and to the rich man who wanted to follow Him, befriending them and loving them by the giving of His time. If He were here today, He would not be grousing about the color of the Starbucks coffee cup or nitpicking about the hidden messages of Teletubbies' Tinky Winky and his handbag. Unbelievers might recognize that we are Christians by our love. But they can also spot insincerity, hypocrisy, and self-promoting agendas masquerading as truth a mile away.

Paul elevated soul winning to a worship art. He channeled his charisma and made himself a servant to all, that he might win more of them, becoming "all things to all people" to populate God's kingdom (1 Corinthians 9:22). The lost don't want your proverbial "righteous selfies," or those pics with inflammatory digs or our puffed-up declarations of how pious we are. They need your authentic love, your support. They need to see that you walk humbly with God. Listen to His cues on how to best represent Him at work and in your personal life.

Keys to Kingdom Living: Practice WWJD ("what would Jesus do") in your workplace, analyze your motives, and pray before speaking.

Doorpost: "The fruit of the righteous is a tree of life." Proverbs 11:30

THE TREASURED GIFT OF LISTENING:
IN YOUR FAMILY RELATIONS

*W*hen the TV talk show *The View* first came out, I was astounded with how difficult it was to follow what was being said. Everyone spoke at once, and hardly anyone yielded the floor. This kind of rude behavior, while apparently popular on reality TV programs these days, is less effective in social situations and is particularly damaging when it comes to family life.

With some trepidation I confess to you that I was bickering with my husband minutes before writing this. I felt like he was not listening to my answers to the questions he was asking. In the contemplation of my words here, I called him and listened to him again and urged him to listen to me. We both struck a respectful compromise to an issue we don't agree on. Yet each of us are certain we were heard. Healthy relationships should be able to withstand some disagreement. But agreement aside, we must listen to others just as we have a need to be heard ourselves.

Our homes should ideally function as sanctuaries, not spaces filled with discontent. We have a need to feel safe inside them, to be loved and understood, even if those under our roof do not agree with everything we say. This kind of environment is fostered when love, respect, and often humility are present in our dealings with each other. In James 1:19 we are told "everyone must be quick to hear, slow to speak, and slow to anger." The order of those actions is quite intentional and runs counter to human nature. Often, we are quick to anger. We're eager to immediately say exactly what we think, and only if we have finished our argument will we be silent. We pretend to listen when in fact we're formulating the next thing we are about to say.

The way we listen—and the act of sometimes just not saying anything—is just as important. We read the telling, yet humorous, tidbit of wisdom in Proverbs 17:28 that "even fools are thought wise when they keep silent; with their mouths shut, they seem intelligent" (NLT). Proverbs also cautions us to make our ears attentive to wisdom and to incline our hearts toward understanding. We are often guilty of inclining our hearts toward antagonizing those with whom we disagree. This might even be unintentional. We need discernment. Rarely is it more important to be right than it is to humble ourselves, listen to the other side, and strike a compromise. We might even need to be open to adopting another viewpoint based on what has been said. People who are all talk close their minds and hearts to other viewpoints and to harmony, putting their relationships at risk and their pride in the driver's seat.

In Titus 3:2, a perfect prescription for equilibrium in relationships urges us "to slander no one, to avoid fighting, and to be kind, always showing gentleness to all people." That may be a tall order and a lofty goal. But the suggestions go a long way in promoting a fertile ground for serenity at home and, more importantly, fostering inner peace. Next time you feel an argument coming on, why not take the fine art of listening to a new level?

Keys to Kingdom Living: Never miss an opportunity to open your ears and close your mouth.

Doorpost: "The one who gives an answer before he listens—this is foolishness and disgrace for him." Proverbs 18:13

THE TREASURED GIFT OF LISTENING: IN OUR FRIENDSHIPS

*W*hen we really listen to another person, it demonstrates that we care about them. We know all too well that the converse of caring about someone is the act of ignoring him or her. We are inclined to put our "ignoring" hat on for telemarketers and door-to-door salesmen, for instance. (Of course, in light of the coronavirus pandemic, the whole door-to-door practice is on the wane.) We might stare right at them, but if they don't capture our interest, we simply bide our time until the words "I'm not interested" can finally be uttered.

It's vitally important to discard our "ignoring" hat when it comes to our personal dealings. And even if we don't truly ignore someone, we need to do more than simply hear what they say; we need to really listen. A girlfriend I know admitted to me that when one long-winded sister calls, she puts the phone on speaker and tidies up her house, sometimes leaving the room for long periods of time, then re-entering the room and offering up an occasional "mm-hmm" so the sister thinks she's been heard, when in fact she has not.

Any friend, whether long-winded or not, still deserves our undivided attention. We're itching to give advice when all the person really wants is a shoulder to cry on. They want you to say, "That must make you feel just terrible." We need to learn to discern when dispensing advice needs to take a back seat to showing love and concern. Whether we have heard the friend's grievance or problem one hundred times before makes no difference in the level of attention we should give to them. What matters most to us will capture our attention.

Many well-meaning listeners assume that advice or wise counsel should accompany any authentic conversation. But advice —especially when unsolicited—is rarely taken, according to a study conducted by *Psychology Today* magazine.[1] In the study, researchers found that people usually resist unsolicited advice and instruction. It did show, though, that they will follow the behaviors of others, especially when these individuals appear to be good. In scenarios with those individuals, reinforcing outcomes stemmed from these behaviors or beliefs. They also found that if one person in a relationship practiced good listening skills, the other was more inclined to pay closer attention to what the other person said to them, modeling the gift of listening that was given to them.

What can we learn from those stats? Your best chance of gaining an audience for your advice is to be the listener you want your friend to be. When we offer this gift to a friend, it shows we care enough to invest in them and demonstrates our love in a tangible way. If, as we listen to problems or grievances, we are sending arrow prayers to the Lord about how to best respond, if a response is called for, we are effectively serving as His hands and feet. When we do that, we're truly loving one another as Jesus loved us (John 13:34).

Keys to Kingdom Living: Give the gift of listening to your friends to demonstrate your love.

Doorpost: "Iron sharpens iron, and one man sharpens another." Proverbs 27:17

THE TREASURED GIFT OF LISTENING:
WHILE IN PRAYER FOR YOUR
MINISTRY

*M*any faithful servants of God structure their schedule around their ministries. For instance, because I have a teenage son with autism, I once structured my responsibilities around blocks of time when I knew he would likely be at school so I was available to work. We may pray about whether we are called to serve in a ministry and be careful calendar builders as we weigh our actual availability against the many things we are interested in doing. Yet we sometimes neglect to meditate and listen for direction on other aspects of our ministries.

How many of you have sat in church and heard of a new ministry starting up that excited you to be a part of it? Pre-COVID, our church announced that it was going to partner with a local hospital to offer church services on the premises for patients and their families. At the time, I was excited to hear about this and signed up immediately to join the team.

I felt like my enthusiasm was a leading from the Lord to be a regular contributor to the weekly needs of the ministry. But something seemed to get in the way of every meeting. When I was finally able to attend one, and saw the needs of that ministry listed, the sentence which read "pray for this service" jumped out at me. The Lord was clear: He wanted me to do that. Though it might not seem like an important box to check off a to-do list or something that would require a large chunk of time, God still clarified for me exactly what He wanted me to do with my spiritual gift set and available time.

Hearing God's voice requires us to listen to small leadings before we dive in headfirst to the proverbial service pool. Beyond praying for the initial green light to serve Him, we need to pray over a variety of aspects of our service. We need to listen for God's direction in big and small things. We should pray regularly for harmony and a spirit of cooperation among all who work in any ministry. We can pray for folks individually, and we can also listen and wait for Him to communicate to us about how to pray for, or possibly contact, that person. Deciding what to do—whether to approach them, and how—should come from God, rather than just taking actions into our own hands. That's especially true if the situation involves a simmering problem or a piece of constructive criticism.

Methods of approaching people remain a crucial part of such conversations. After moving to Los Angeles, my husband and I visited a new church. As we approached our car, we noticed someone frantically running toward us on the street where we had parked. Somewhat alarmed, we hurried to find the car key, not exactly sure what was happening. The man, out of breath, had come from church and said he wanted to meet and greet us before we left. Though he clearly meant well, it was a startling encounter that reeked of desperation. It felt more unsettling than welcoming and, needless to say, it did not entice us to return. I doubt he listened to God and instead dove into the pool. We become more effective ambassadors for Christ when we open our ears and wait to hear from Him.

Keys to Kingdom Living: Listen for leadings from God about all aspects of ministry.

Doorpost: "The LORD says, 'I will guide you along the best pathway for your life. I will advise you and watch over you.'" Psalm 32:8 (NLT)

THE TREASURED GIFT OF LISTENING:
IN YOUR QUIET TIME

*O*ften in my quiet time or prayer, my attention drifts. I believe all human beings succumb to distraction when they pray. Oh, we start off well enough, intending to praise God, thank Him, offer confession, and then petition to Him. But minutes into the process, at least for me, I end up traveling down a rabbit's warren of distraction. I might end up fretting whether to buy a free-range chicken or a pork roast for dinner or some other to-do list item.

Sadly, the "spirit is willing, but the flesh is weak," as Jesus pointed out when speaking to the disciples in the Garden of Gethsemane, as recorded in Matthew 26:41. In this event, Jesus took His remaining eleven disciples with Him (Judas had already left the fold) but took only three a little farther into the garden with Him. There, he explained that He was overwhelmed with sorrow and instructed them to stay and keep watch. Instead, they ended up falling asleep.

Before we judge too harshly, how often do we succumb to distractions during our quiet time? When our spirit is willing, but our schedules beckon, our selfish pursuits interfere, and busyness gets a foothold? If you are like me, the answer is, "More often than I care to admit!" But you can take steps to quiet your mind and our environment so God's voice is not drowned out.

The first step toward more effective listening to God is to make sure you have quiet. If your home is noisy, sequester yourself in a closet or bathroom or slip on some noise-cancelling headphones. You can also pick a time when everyone is gone or asleep. Rather than just rushing into His presence, it's a good idea to read or listen to something inspirational from a CD, Bible, or a book.

After you have finished reading, reflect on what you read and ask God what He has to say to you specifically about the passages or ideas presented to you that day. This is one of the most challenging aspects of quiet time but one of the most imperative. Because we are constantly bombarded with music, images, pictures, text messages, and the like, we are not as comfortable with silence as we ought to be. But we need to give God space to respond. Some days will yield more response than others, but by building this time in, we keep our dialogue going with Him. A real relationship involves speaking and listening, and the relationship we enjoy with God is no different in that area, even if we can't see Him.

Keys to Kingdom Living: By carving out margin and setting our focus in our quiet time with God, we provide Him with access to our lives. As a result, we allow Him to help shape and guide thoughts and actions.

Doorpost: "Then He said [to Elijah], 'Go out and stand on the mountain in the LORD's presence.' . . . A great and mighty wind was tearing at the mountains and was shattering cliffs . . . but the Lord was not in the wind. After the wind there was an earthquake, but the LORD was not in the earthquake. After the earthquake there was a fire, but the LORD was not in the fire. And after the fire there was a voice, a soft whisper." 1 Kings 19:11–12

THE TREASURED GIFT OF LISTENING:
WHAT GOD ALWAYS DOES

I have a number of close friends and even occasional acquaintances who regularly ask me to pray for and with them. Sometimes I am asked to offer wise counsel. Of course, my own counsel is worthless, so I always ask the Lord to provide discernment in these situations as opposed to just flapping my lips on the fly. But I must confess that I do not have total recall when it comes to the whos, whats, and whens of these convos.

But God not only can remember all these details—He does. And it's not just that He keeps them all in His head. We are told in Revelation 5:8 that the prayers of all the saints are kept in golden bowls. Our prayers become His incense. When I think of the little scraps of paper with prayer requests scribbled on them that end up in the trash, it gives me pause to think what awesome reverence the Lord holds for our humble petitions. I love how He provides us with a visual of the openness of a bowl, making the petitions accessible and visible. It's also telling that they are housed in a container made of such a precious metal. It is my hope and prayer that one day I can lay my eyes on this precious vessel.

How often do we turn to everyone but God until our situation seems hopeless and unbearable? Often, in that moment, we finally take our problem to Him as the last, rather than first, resort. God should be our first stop in crisis so that His peace will reign in the midst of trauma and disorder. We should eagerly desire His hand to be all over every problematic situation in our lives, whether it be big or small.

What a gift to be able, in your ultimate time of need, to go to someone who knows your situation and heart's desire before you even begin to utter it. Even though some people maintain that God simply doesn't understand their situations, the truth is that no one understands any situation more than God. He even tells us that Jesus is the ultimate empathizer and that He was "tested in every way as we are, yet without sin," according to Hebrews 4:15. In light of that, we can be assured that our responses in prayer will be godly and trustworthy.

Thankfully, God never tries to finish your sentences, looks at His watch, or checks His iPhone for text messages from other Christ-followers. You always have His undivided attention. He's never planning what to say next, and He knew of your petition before you even made it. You don't need to worry about being clear or filling in every detail. Eloquent or lofty words aren't needed to impress Him. And even if your thoughts wander as you pray, God continues to track with you. He will patiently wait as your mind wanders and be right there when you redirect your thoughts. It's no wonder these petitions are kept in a golden bowl —the precious attention from God elevates them to that of a beautiful offering from our heart to His!

Keys to Kingdom Living: God is a champion listener who has no equal.

Doorpost: "The eyes of the LORD are on the righteous and His ears are open to their request. But the face of the LORD is against those who do what is evil." 1 Peter 3:12

WEEK 10: PRECIOUS SCENTS

PRECIOUS SCENTS: AND MATTERS OF THE HEART

The most common aroma wafting from inside many Protestant churches today might be that of robust drip coffee. But since the edicts of Exodus, incense has been an integral part of the ceremonial rituals surrounding the honor required from the priests.

Though it's rare today to find incense burning in a sacred space, its origin dates back to the Holy Place and the Holy of Holies as recorded in the Old Testament. At that time, God commanded the priests to burn incense on the golden altar during the same time that the burnt offerings were to be made. The incense itself was made of four coveted spices. They included the precious frankincense, once considered a holy temple fragrance never to be duplicated for outside use. The punishment for doing so was exile, according to Exodus 30.

The symbolism of incense is rooted in the idea that prayers, like the airy fragrance, are wafting up to heaven. Incense, like prayer, relies on a catalyst to get things moving upward. In our prayer life, catalysts vary as much as our prayers. We may feel God's greatness in the viewing of a rainbow and declare His majesty. The moment we hold our infant in our arms, that action may prompt a prayer of gratitude. If we break one of God's commandments, we might be compelled to offer a prayer of confession. When we are suffering from the loss of a loved one, we might cry out to God for comfort. And in the moments where we are faced with painful decisions, we beg God for wisdom and help in our times of deepest need.

Whatever the catalyst is that ignites a spark that prompts prayer, the sweet fragrance of all our petitions is highly pleasing to the Lord. Though earthly smoke may dissipate, our sincere petitions are so precious to Him that He preserves each one like the keepsakes He sees them to be. Isn't it wonderful? God not only never tires of hearing from us, He deeply treasures and curates our dialogue with Him.

When we pray to God and He receives our heartfelt prayers, we are communing with Him in a uniquely sweet way. But when we worry or complain or blame circumstances for our frustration, pain, or sadness, something else happens. We're unable to generate the pleasant aroma so integral to the child/parent relationship that our Father God designed for our mutual enjoyment. We essentially deny ourselves that access. Our rank fragrance is more akin to that of someone in need of a good cleansing. We need to continually cultivate the spark of opportunity as we transform our concerns into the gratitude-filled prayers God intended them to become.

Keys to Kingdom Living: May our reliance on God produce a sweet fragrance.

Doorpost: "May my prayer be set before You as incense, the raising of my hands as the evening offering." Psalm 141:2

PRECIOUS SCENTS: AS SACRIFICIAL GIFTS TO THE CHRIST CHILD

*W*hile still nestled in his humble bed of straw in Bethlehem, the baby Jesus received three gifts from the wise men, two of which were fragrant oils of frankincense and myrrh. These precious gifts were costly because of their expensive ingredients but were also highly significant of the life Jesus was born to lead.

Frankincense is a symbol of His priestly role. Used exclusively in the temple to blend a holy aroma, we read in Leviticus 16:12–13 that the cloud of incense may cover the mercy seat for the Lord. We know from many passages in Exodus and Leviticus that a cloud visually represented the presence of the Lord. The oil required a monetary sacrifice to purchase but also symbolized a sacrifice of a deeper meaning.

Jesus was our ultimate High Priest and the ultimate sacrifice. We read in Hebrews 2:17 that He was made "like His brothers [and sisters] in every way, so that He could become a merciful and faithful high priest in service to God " His life purpose as a living sacrifice provided the required restitution for atonement of our disobedience. He also intercedes for us to His Father as our High Priest until the day we are permanently and completely restored in the New Jerusalem.

Myrrh, used in death and embalming, represents Jesus's role as the ultimate sacrifice and a "ransom for many" (Mark 10:45). It signified the sufferings of His humanity as God and man. Myrrh was also revered for its healing properties. It was used to anoint the furnishings and artifacts in the temple, as well as priests including Aaron and kings such as Solomon. Myrrh was described as a most holy oil, and anything it touched became holy as well, as we read in Exodus 30:29.

You might be wondering about the significance of all this. Theologian Emanuel Swedenborg proposed that the gift of frankincense represents the offering of the truth in our minds about Jesus. The gift of myrrh represents the offering during the service and a lifting of our hands to Jesus. As we ponder God's Word and the truths it imparts, we indeed offer up the sweet fragrance of worship and adoration. It is destined to reach and bless the King of Kings and Lord of Lords. And when we lay down our own lives in service to Him, offering ourselves to Him as His hands and feet, we indeed die to ourselves. Our old life is buried and we become alive in Christ.

As we contemplate the precious gifts given to Jesus by the wise men, we can't escape the truth about not only what they represent but of what they foretold. The gifts themselves were purchased at great cost. They were given to the One who would pay the ultimate price with the only gift He brought into the world—that of His life. What a gift God has given us in Jesus Christ!

Our lives are gifts too. As we become more like Jesus, are we willing to give our own lives as a ransom for many? Are we willing to lay down our lives for our friends, to search for that ninety-ninth sheep who is lost? When we are, that scent of sacrifice is sure to please our Father God.

Keys to Kingdom Living: Will we choose to be an aromatic offering to Him and die to ourselves?

Doorpost: "And walk in love, as the Messiah also loved us and gave Himself for us, a sacrificial and fragrant offering to God." Ephesians 5:2

PRECIOUS SCENTS: MARY'S COSTLY, MISUNDERSTOOD SACRIFICE

As a young girl flipping through magazines, I remember spotting an ad for a perfume by Jean Patou called Joy. The tagline for the ad read, "The most costly perfume in the world." I tried to imagine what might be used to make the perfume so expensive. I later read that for a short two-week span in the summer, the 10,600 flowers required for a single bottle of Joy are harvested in Grasse, France. I remember thinking about the term "costly" as opposed to "expensive" for the first time, realizing that cost isn't something that is solely limited to monetary expenditure. Imagine a pile of 10,600 flowers in a heap next to a single-ounce container of their precious drops.

One of today's most expensive perfumes costs an astounding $215,000 for 16.9 ounces. So when we read in John 12:3–5 of Mary's sacrificial act of pouring out the equivalent of a year's salary of fragrance, we can imagine the shock and turmoil. The pint used for the act (according to Scripture) was worth about 300 denarii, which, at the time, was worth a year's pay for someone employed on the level of agricultural worker.

This ancient oil with the essence of nard, a precious fragrance, was what Mary poured over the feet of Jesus, using her own hair to dry them. The oil, also called spikenard, is an amber-colored essential oil cultivated from a flowering plant of the valerian family found in the Himalayas. Many of those who witnessed Mary's selfless act, including Judas, misunderstood it. He described the act as extravagant and wasteful and tried to point out that the money could have been used for the poor.

While there is a kernel of truth in that statement, what really stinks here (pun intended) is that Judas didn't care one bit for the poor. In fact, we learn in Scripture that Judas was in charge of the coffers and helped himself to the funds as he pleased without any regard for their highest and best use. Mary, no doubt, was the one who procured the expensive oil. Mary demonstrated through her sacrifice that she was all-in for Jesus. She sacrificed the monetary investment to lavish her love on Jesus, and that was all that mattered in that moment: her heart filled with total love. All the costly ingredients sacrificed in making the oil and the sacrifice Mary made in buying it pale in comparison to the sacrifice made by the One who sacrificed His life for all mankind. She also fulfilled Scripture by symbolically preparing His body, as He states in John 12:7.

Sometimes God calls us to give in ways that may appear ridiculous to outsiders. I remember once being prompted by God to give someone I knew a large sum of money. The recipient had not asked for anything. It was a person who had done some occasional work for me. No illuminating reasons for me to give this money were revealed to me by God. The only thing I knew for sure was that she and her family were very poor and struggled to make ends meet. I still to this day don't know why God compelled me to give that amount, that one time, in that moment. I only knew that I was to do it. What we do always know is that His ways are not ours. But when God prompts us to sacrifice, ours is not to question why!

Keys to Kingdom Living: Listen to God and act in matters of extravagant giving.

Doorpost: "Set [your] hope on . . . God, who richly provides us with all things to enjoy. . . . Do what is good, . . . be rich in good works, . . . be generous, willing to share." 1 Timothy 6:17–18

PRECIOUS SCENTS: EMBALMING THE
LIVING GOD

The crisp smell of freshness is unmistakable. A field of blooming fresh flowers, fresh bread out of the oven, a baby fresh from a bath—these aromas delight all who take them in. But what about the smell of dead, dried-up flowers, moldy bread, or a corpse? Odors from these things yield far different reactions.

Inarguably, life and death could not be more different from one another. Yet only the King of Kings and Lord of Lords could take the stench of His own sacrificial death and turn it into eternal life for all who believe in Him. As was the case with other entombed Jewish bodies of the day, the wrapped and embalmed body of Jesus lay in the tomb—but only for three days short days prior to His miraculous resurrection. Thanks to two wealthy followers, the proper embalming ointments, linen clothes, and a sizable tomb were donated for His temporary use, although no one at the time had any inkling of the glorious outcome of the seemingly tragic series of events.

We can certainly understand the practical reason embalming bodies became customary. But reasons for embalming a dead body aren't specifically mentioned in Scripture. However, our physical, mortal death is also accompanied by the death of our moral corruption. Indeed, a Christian at the end of his or her life can rest assured that the good fight was fought (2 Timothy 4:7) and the victory is won through Jesus Christ (1 Corinthians 15:57).

Perhaps the application of the sacred oils in some ways is intended to symbolize how we are sealed in Christ. Maybe it's designed to preserve us in a holding pattern until the day our souls are reunited with our new bodies in the New Jerusalem. "Look, I am making everything new!" John writes of Jesus's bold declaration in Revelation 21:5. Beginning with His own resurrection, Jesus sealed the deal for sinners reeking of their vile misdeeds and declared them fresh, new creations in Christ. What a blessing this is for all who belong to Him!

Of course we know the Potter doesn't need the old clay to work His miraculous transformation. All He needs are willing hearts open to the receipt of His grace, ready for a fulfilling life of obedience. And sacrifice, along with commitment, releases a fresh scent of gratitude for all He has done for us. When we bloom where He has planted us, surely the sweet fragrance that results will attract the "walking dead" who are ripe for conversion. That's our cue to step out in boldness with open arms to witness to them and, ideally, welcome them into the flower field of believers.

Keys to Kingdom Living: We can be confident we are preserved until we are made new again in the New Jerusalem.

Doorpost: "Nicodemus also came [with Joseph of Arimathea], bringing a mixture of about 75 pounds of myrrh and aloes. Then they took Jesus' body and wrapped it in linen cloths with the aromatic spices, according to the burial custom of the Jews." John 19:39–40

PRECIOUS SCENTS: THE SWEET
FRAGRANCE OF CHRISTIANS

*W*hen I visited Rwanda on a mission trip years ago, one of the first adjustments I had to make in my attitude was toward the natural aroma emanating from the villagers, who had little access to water. Bathing was more of a weekly rather than daily ritual for them. Because the culture is one where deep triple hugs are the order of the day, my colleagues and I took to placing essential oils under our noses early on in the trip. This would combat the odor—a blend of wood smoke and natural, earthy body odor—that we were unaccustomed to smelling.

However, as the week stretched on and the inner beauty of the villagers became more evident, we became accustomed to their scent. Even as I write this, my mind travels back to those times—and though it sounds crazy, I remember the smell of the people with a wistful fondness. When I think about the sweet inner fragrance of the Rwandan Christians and contrast it with the commercial fragrance Unbreakable Bond, created by Khloé Kardashian and Lamar Odom back in 2011, it gives me pause. The couple has since filed for divorce; apparently the fragrance outlasted the relationship, which in itself has gone rancid.

Our fragrance lingers, too, wherever we go, long after the impact of our words. We can lecture our kids until we are blue in the face about telling the truth, but if they hear us lying to a friend and saying we're busy when we're not, is our fragrance sweet or wildly decomposed? But when we heed the leadings of our

Wonderful Counselor as we make that caring phone call, send that special card, or give that warm hug, we emanate a scent that is highly pleasing to God and educational to all who witness it.

Our fragrance, like those we spray onto ourselves, requires more than a one-time spritz. Back in my reporting days I wrote an article about fragrance layering. The premise was that you would use a scented cleanser, followed by an application of a scented lotion, and finish with three spritzes of cologne. By implementing that carefully curated trifecta, you supposedly could walk around for most of the day assured of smelling great.

Christians can do the same. We can cleanse ourselves daily by confessing our sins to God. We can apply lotion, accepting the layer of armor God puts on us, which protects against any opposition that may come between us and God's plans and purposes. Finally, we can spray on the sweet aroma of Jesus, receiving His love and passing it on as we behave as He would in every situation we face throughout the day. By keeping up our fragrance layering, people will begin to notice and wonder what we are wearing and may even want to secure it for themselves. What greater legacy can we leave behind than helping to bring others into the fragrant fold?

Keys to Kingdom Living: Embrace the daily practice of layering the sweet fragrance of Jesus so others will be attracted to His love and amazing grace.

Doorpost: "For to God we are the fragrance of Christ among those who are being saved and among those who are perishing." 2 Corinthians 2:15

PRECIOUS SCENTS: ARE WE STINKERS OR BLOOMERS?

*Y*ou may have heard of the corpse flower, the Indonesian plant that rarely blooms, and when it does, it's only for a short time. While it blooms, it emits a strong odor similar to rotting meat or, as its name suggests, a rotting corpse. While you may think that all pollinators would be repelled by the stench, the truth is a select few are gamers for the project. Dung beetles, flesh flies, and other carnivorous insects are the primary pollinators for the corpse flower. The plant actually imitates a dead animal to attract these bugs.

Unfortunately, Christians who complain and bicker and behave in a divisive manner are stinking up the flower field of the saints. The bitter aroma they exude is not attracting nonbelievers into the fold but instead sends them running for the hills. You may have heard this famous quote: "I like your Christ, I do not like your Christians. Your Christians are so unlike your Christ."

That painful truth stings, since we all know our share of corpse flowers as well as lilies. Stories of church leaders embezzling, womanizing, molesting children, and organizing bombings do little to attract already skeptical agnostics and atheists to the Christian faith.

Unlike the corpse flower that cannot alter its existence, the stinky Christian is given the power to change from within, as long as the desire is there. Every Christian makes a daily choice to trust God and de-emphasize the circumstances that bring them down.

In my closet I have a message emblazoned near the ceiling: "This is the day the Lord has made; let us rejoice and be glad in it" (Psalm 118:24). This verse reminds me that every day is a gift for God, whether we acknowledge it or not. Unfortunately, this verse is often misinterpreted. We don't have to be glad about what is in a day. If a loved one dies or our home is foreclosed on, we don't have to declare false joy. We are simply called to acknowledge that everything God makes is good—not to deny our feelings about our pain but instead to say, "I trust in God in the day He made."

I'm not saying this is an easy task. But I do believe that when we stand with God in our tough circumstances and choose to remain aligned with God throughout them, the most beautiful resulting fragrance produces unimaginable results. It is highly personalized, and no two will be alike. When Christians rise above their circumstances and can testify to their ability to overcome, the stinkers take notice. The fragrant few commend and encourage others. God honors and will someday reward them.

Keys to Kingdom Living: Choose to emanate a sweet aroma every day, no matter what circumstances you may face in the day.

Doorpost: "Because of Christ, we give off a sweet scent rising to God, which is recognized by those on the way of salvation—an aroma redolent with life." 2 Corinthians 2:16-17 (MSG)

PRECIOUS SCENTS: DISTILLING AND
REFINING OUR FRAGRANCE

*V*ery few people go out to their garden, rub themselves with a flower, and hope to smell good the rest of the day. Because there's no way they will. Consumers usually buy a fragrance primarily because the tedious process, combined with the vast amount of ingredients needed, is such a huge undertaking. Commercial fragrances are a combination of a variety of organic raw floral and plant material. These raw materials are dissolved in a solvent, resulting in the creation of the desired aromatic compounds. Eventually the solvent is removed, and the remaining mixture is the stuff of which the ultimate fragrance is made, bottled, packaged, and sold.

Whenever a fragrance is made, a vessel is required that can literally take the heat, as heating the compound may be necessary in the scent-making process. A Christian is the vessel God uses to create a sweet fragrance, which results from obedience and devotion to God. Mature Christians understand they will face trials and adapt themselves to take the heat through faith, the power of prayer, and support from fellow vessels. They give God their raw materials—their talents, their energy, their schedules, and their agendas. God permits their submersion into the solvent of hardship to extract their essences.

Our vessels take the heat and yield the fragrance they were born to create. But creating any fragrance requires time, patience, and the knowledge that each step brings the comprehensive process closer to completion. Being mindful of this when we are in the middle of seemingly unbearable adversity that will further our "scent-making" process can help spur us on to complete the race God has marked out for us (Hebrews 12:1).

On days when I imagine what heaven will be like, I wonder about the fragrance aspect. When all the saints are gathered in the New Jerusalem, I can't help but imagine the aromatic environment we will enjoy. The hard-won perfume of each believer will mingle in exquisite harmony with the scents of all the other saints. Imagine this, intermingled with notes of our heartfelt prayers from the golden bowl and the precious mixture of frankincense and myrrh. What a feast for the senses this will be!

When we use our mind's eye to imagine eternity, the resulting hope can spur us on, even when life truly stinks. Concentration camp survivor, psychiatrist, and author Viktor Frankl tells of an ill fellow inmate at Auschwitz who was near her life's end in his famous book *Man's Search for Meaning*. Surprisingly, she expressed gratitude to him regarding the suffering she had endured. "In my former life, I was spoiled and did not take spiritual accomplishments seriously."[1] Outside the shabby hut of their confines sat a chestnut tree. The woman told him that the tree, the only friend in her loneliness, spoke to her, saying, "I am here, I am here, I am life. Eternal life."[2]

Keys to Kingdom Living: Permit your vessel to take the heat as it transforms raw materials into the unique, sweet fragrance only each Christ-follower can produce.

Doorpost: "How delightful your love is. . . . Your love is much better than wine, and the fragrance of your perfume than any balsam." Song of Solomon 4:10–14

ACKNOWLEDGMENTS

As I close the door on this final installment of my door devotion trilogy, I'm feeling a myriad of emotions. It feels good to have completed what God put on my heart to accomplish five or so years ago. But it's a bittersweet feeling as well, knowing that this particular book project has come to an end. Fortunately, God is always doing something new in our lives. He put a new project on my heart last spring even before *The Vault Door* was completed. My latest non-book "door" is a new podcast! "His GPS for Your SOS" has opened up an entire new area of ministry for me and expanded my international audience. It uploads weekly and always clocks in under ten minutes!

As has been the case with my other books, each "door" I would work on at any given point in my life revealed a significance within that particular time frame. My "side door" of parenting a severely autistic child inspired my first book. And I experienced a significant descent through a "trap door" I smugly thought I was beyond facing as I wrapped up my second door devotional. This third book, a treasure trove of truths and promises from God, is being released at a time when many "locked down" people (myself included) need to lock some things up.

It's my hope and prayer that your vault overhaul will be as fruitful as mine has been. Whether you are in lockdown as you read it or you are at the zenith of experiencing your freedom in the world as well as in Christ, you will find precious jewels worth securing. As of this writing, much about our earthly future definitely remains in limbo, but we know we can trust God to deliver on His promises for the long view.

And now for the shout-outs! Many thanks once again to the fabulous Jody Skinner at Skinner Self-Publishing Services. I'm so grateful for her keen editing as well as her infinite patience with all of my technological deficiencies. And to Leona Hunt, who graciously checked every Bible verse for accuracy, I offer my heartfelt gratitude. To Maryam Siahatgar for designing yet another compelling cover, thank you.

A bounty of thanks as well to my husband of thirty-seven years, Ben. His limitless financial support of my ministry as well as his unmerited distribution of grace regarding my own substantial shortcomings is nothing short of miraculous. As we move through life, I realize that the more we model the grace dispensed to us by our Lord and Savior Jesus Christ, the better positioned we are to receive it in our time of need, as we are reminded in Hebrews 4:16. I don't know about you, but I feel like I need all the grace I can get these days!

And to you, the readers, who have supported me and the ministry God laid on my heart so many years ago, thank you so much for your support. May your lives and your vaults overflow with abundant blessings from the Lord for many years to come.

ABOUT THE AUTHOR

Cindy LaFavre Yorks is an award-winning writer, podcaster, and author of three door devotion books. After decades of covering fashion and the red carpet for national newspapers and magazines, she traded in her stilettos for sandals and entered through the door of special needs parenting. Married to husband Ben for thirty-seven years, she is now the empty-nested mother of two sons and lives in Orange County, California.

Connect with Cindy at www.cindyyorks.com. She posts daily encouragement on Instagram and can also be found on Facebook. Her biweekly podcast, "His GPS for Your SOS," uploads weekly to a variety of hosting sites.

NOTES

2. IN THE VAULT: INVENTORYING YOUR VALUABLES

1. "Saint Patrick and the Easter Fire," Catholic Books and Media | Pauline Books & Media | Daughters of St. Paul, 2017, http://www.pauline.org/Pauline-Books-Media-Blog/ArticleID/3017/Saint-Patrick-and-the-Easter-Fire.
2. Nate Loper, "Prayer of St. Patrick," Life, legend, and lighting of fires..., March 17, 2016, http://www.genesisscience.org/prayer-of-st-patrick/.

3. IN THE VAULT: KEYS TO A SOLID, FORT-KNOX LOCKUP

1. "U.S. Department of the Treasury." 2010. Currency & Coins: Fort Knox Bullion Depository. November 13, 2010. https://www.treasury.gov/about/education/Pages/fort-knox.aspx.

5. IN THE VAULT: BOLSTERING YOUR SECURITY

1. Chang, Rachel. 2020. "Michael Fagan: The Intruder Who Broke Into Buckingham Palace." Biography.com. A&E Networks Television. November 16, 2020. https://www.biography.com/news/michael-fagan-queen-elizabeth-buckingham-palace-intruder.

3. THE INVESTMENT OF SPIRITUAL TRAINING: THE PRINCIPLE OF OVERLOAD

1. Mike McCombs, "Beaufort's CJ Cummings Smashes American, World Records on Way to USA Weightlifting Men's National Championship," The State, August 16, 2015, https://www.thestate.com/sports/article31264247.html.
2. McCombs, "Beaufort's CJ Cummings Smashes American, World Records on Way to USA Weightlifting Men's National Championship."

7. THE INVESTMENT OF SPIRITUAL TRAINING: THE PRINCIPLE OF REST

1. Gil Student, "What's Wrong with Texting on Shabbat? A Halachic Analysis," *Jewish Action*, spring 2002, accessed November 17, 2020, https://jewishaction.com/religion/whats-wrong-with-texting-on-shabbat-a-halachic-analysis-2/.

2. SEVEN KEY VERSES: JOHN 13:34

1. Oswald Chambers, "Love One Another," *My Utmost for His Highest* (1934), May 11th entry, My Utmost for His Highest (website), https://utmost.org/love-one-another/.
2. Chambers, "Love One Another."

3. INVESTING IN SECURITY: IN THE TOTALITY OF OUR REDEMPTION

1. Kate Brumback, "'I'm Not Too Ashamed': 85-Year-Old Jewel Thief Reflects on Life," *Business Insider*, January 31, 2016, https://www.businessinsider.com/i-was-a-thief-85-year-old-jewel-pilfering-woman-reflects-on-her-life-of-crime-2016-1.

5. VALUABLE LESSONS FROM CREATION: A ROOSTER'S REMINDER

1. Karl Smallwood, "Why Do Roosters Crow?" *Business Insider*, February 3, 2015, https://www.businessinsider.com/why-roosters-crow-2015-2?r=UK.

3. CONTEMPLATING THE AWE OF GOD: SEAS, WALKING ON LIFE'S SEAS

1. Paul Piff and Dacher Keltner, "Why Do We Experience Awe?" *The New York Times*, May 22, 2015, https://www.nytimes.com/2015/05/24/opinion/sunday/why-do-we-experience-awe.html.
2. Piff and Keltner, "Why Do We Experience Awe?"

2. NOT-SO-LITTLE THINGS TO LOCK UP: A LOVING TOUCH

1. Suzanne Degges-White, "Skin Hunger: Why You Need to Feed Your Hunger for Contact;
Research into the Psychological Benefits of a Warm Embrace," January 7, 2015, https://www.psychologytoday.com/ca/blog/lifetime-connections/201501/skin-hunger-why-you-need-feed-your-hunger-contact.
2. Maia Szalavitz, "Touching Empathy: Lack of Physical Affection Can Actually Kill Babies," *Psychology Today*, March 1, 2010, https://www.psychologytoday.com/ca/blog/born-love/201003/touching-empathy.
3. Szalavitz, "Touching Empathy."

1. THE TREASURED GIFT OF LISTENING: TO GOD IN THE QUIET MOMENTS

1. Carl Sandburg, "Fog," Poetry Foundation (website), accessed November 24, 2020, https://www.poetryfoundation.org/poems/45032/fog-56d2245d7b36c.

4. THE TREASURED GIFT OF LISTENING: IN OUR FRIENDSHIPS

1. Thomas G. Plante, "Giving People Advice Rarely Works, This Does: Go Against Your Instincts to Influence Others," *Psychology Today*, July 15, 2014, https://www.psychologytoday.com/ca/blog/do-the-right-thing/201407/giving-people-advice-rarely-works-does.

7. PRECIOUS SCENTS: DISTILLING AND REFINING OUR FRAGRANCE

1. Viktor E. Frankl, *Man's Search for Meaning: An Introduction to Logotherapy* (1946), 4th ed., trans. Ilse Lasch (Boston: Beacon Press, 1992), 78, https://edisciplinas.usp.br/pluginfile.php/3403095/mod_resource/content/1/56ViktorFrankl_Mans%20Search.pdf.
2. Frankl, *Man's Search for Meaning*, 78.